EMBRACE, EMPOWER, ENGAGE, CHALLENGE, COACH, CELEBRATE

E3C3

THE SIX CORE ELEMENTS OF ELEVATED LEADERSHIP

MARK MULLEN

E3C3: The Six Core Elements of Elevated Leadership
Copyright © 2024 by Mark Mullen

All rights reserved. No part of this publication may be reproduced, distributed, or transmitted in any form or by any means, including photocopying, recording, or other electronic or mechanical methods, without the prior written permission of the author, except in the case of brief quotations embodied in critical reviews and certain other non-commercial uses permitted by copyright law.

Tellwell Talent
www.tellwell.ca

ISBN
978-1-7-7962526-7 (Hardcover)
978-1-7-7962525-0 (Paperback)
978-1-7-7962527-4 (eBook)

TABLE OF CONTENTS

Introduction v

PART ONE - BASE CAMP

Chapter 1:   A Leader Who Made a Difference (Jim the GM) 1
Chapter 2:   Birth of E3C3 7
Chapter 3:   Rainier 10
Chapter 4:   Beware the Leadership Void 16

PART TWO - ASCENT

Chapter 5:   Filling the Leadership Voids 27
Chapter 6:   Embrace 30
Chapter 7:   Empower 49
Chapter 8:   Engage 62
Chapter 9:   Challenge 73
Chapter 10: Coach 82
Chapter 11: Celebrate 94

PART THREE - SUMMIT

Chapter 12: Answering the Call to Elevated Leadership 109
Chapter 13: Implementing Elevated Leadership 125
Chapter 14: Take Action 139

APPENDICES

Appendix I:	Top Ten Leadership Development Assessments	147
Appendix II:	E3C3 Self-Assessment: Leading Yourself	150
Appendix III:	E3C3 Self-Assessment: Leading Others	158
Appendix IV:	E3C3 Self-Assessment: Leading Other Leaders	167
Appendix V:	Recommended Development Actions: Leading Yourself with E3C3	175
Appendix VI:	Recommended Development Actions: Leading Others with E3C3	184
Appendix VII:	Recommended Development Actions: Leading Other Leaders with E3C3	193

INTRODUCTION

From the beginning of my career, I've been driven by a deep passion for leadership, particularly in the realm of leadership development. This passion is rooted in a core belief: Effective leadership is the most critical factor in shaping organizational performance, employee engagement, and individual well-being. This conviction has guided my career and fueled my mission to help individuals, teams, and organizations unlock their leadership potential. This book, *E3C3: The Six Core Elements of Elevated Leadership*, is the culmination of that mission, and I'm excited to share it with you.

Effective leadership development is a critical driver of business success. Companies that invest in well-designed programs often experience significant returns, including improved financial performance, enhanced employee engagement, and higher retention rates. Organizations with strong leadership development are frequently among the top performers in their industry.

However, despite substantial investments in leadership development, many programs fall short of their objectives. Common reasons for this include misalignment with organizational goals, a lack of sustained impact, and insufficient follow-up support. These shortcomings can lead to disengaged employees, productivity losses, and high turnover, resulting in substantial costs for organizations. To overcome these challenges, leadership development initiatives must be closely aligned with the organization's culture, reinforced through practical application, and regularly evaluated to ensure lasting impact and meaningful change.

This is where *E3C3: The Six Core Elements of Elevated Leadership* comes into play. Unlike many leadership development approaches, E3C3 is designed to be simple, practical, and scalable, addressing the common pitfalls of traditional programs. The Six Core Elements of Elevated Leadership provide a structured yet flexible framework that empowers leaders at all levels to develop their potential, drive engagement, and enhance organizational performance. Through this book, you will learn how to apply these elements effectively, ensuring that your leadership development efforts yield meaningful and lasting results.

I have always admired and sought to emulate leaders who elevate those they lead to higher levels of success—I call them Elevated Leaders. Throughout my career, I've had the privilege of witnessing such leaders in action, working with them, observing them, and partnering with them. What I realized was that their success wasn't due to any secret formula or rare talent; it was rooted in something much simpler and more practical. They consistently demonstrated what I have come to identify as the Six Core Elements of Elevated Leadership, and they inspired others to do the same. In this book, you'll meet some of these remarkable leaders through the personal accounts I share. You'll see how they have applied and scaled these Six Core Elements to increase engagement, foster accountability, and build an inclusive leadership culture rooted in trust, respect, and accountability. My hope is that their stories will inspire you to do the same.

E3C3: The Six Core Elements of Elevated Leadership is unlike any other leadership book you're likely to read. It blends personal reflection and storytelling with practical guidance. I share my experiences, the lessons I've learned from Elevated Leaders, and how they inspired the writing of this book. It's also a practical guide that you, your team, and your organization can use to build and sustain an Elevated Leadership culture.

Part One – Base Camp

In Part One of this book, I reflect on the people in our lives and careers who have made a positive, lasting difference. These Elevated Leaders have reached the summit before us, sharing their lessons and helping us achieve higher levels of success. I share my own experience with one such leader, Jim, a general manager whose guidance profoundly shaped my leadership approach. Much of what I learned from him is contained in this book.

I also share the experiences that led to the discovery of the Six Core Elements and how, while climbing a mountain, I found the inspiration and validation to write about them.

I stress the importance of recognizing leadership voids within ourselves, our teams, and our organizations. These voids can arise at any time and in any place, potentially hindering our progress toward our goals and our summit. We'll explore what these voids are and their negative impact. It is mission-critical to pause, assess, and identify any leadership voids to prevent or fill them before they impede our progress.

Part Two - Ascent

In Part Two, I argue that no single leader or select group of leaders can fill all these voids. It takes collective effort from everyone on the team. Elevated Leadership is inclusive leadership, where everyone plays a role in developing leadership potential in themselves and others. This necessitates that our leadership development efforts include everyone in the organization. You can accomplish this with E3C3 Leadership.

Many leadership development efforts fail to produce the desired results because they are often too complex, costly, and difficult to scale sufficiently and effectively. With Elevated Leadership, less is more. It provides a simple, practical, and scalable approach centered on the Six Core Elements. Chapters Six through Eleven offer a glimpse of E3C3 in action, with real examples of how leaders have integrated these Six Core Elements and the impact they've had. These stories will help you understand how to apply them effectively.

Part Three - Summit

With this 'orientation' to E3C3 and the Six Core Elements complete, we begin the ascent. As your guide, I provide a route map with steps that must be completed to build the foundation of an Elevated Leadership culture, upon which all leadership development rests. Leadership development doesn't have to be complicated. In the final chapter, I offer a simple, practical, and scalable approach to reaching the summit by implementing E3C3 and putting the Six Core Elements into practice across your entire organization.

PART ONE
BASE CAMP

CHAPTER ONE

A Leader Who Made a Difference (Jim the GM)

Can you think of a leader who has made a positive difference in your life or career? Perhaps it was a parent or relative, a teacher, a coach, a pastor, or a boss. I am sure you can. My question for you is this: What was it about that person who was so influential and impactful? Was it their personality, abilities, perceived success, station in life, intelligence, charisma, or how they carried themself? Chances are there was something about them you connected with on an intellectual, emotional, and perhaps even a spiritual level that caused you to say to yourself, "That is a person whom I would be willing to follow." I can recall a few people who have had that impact on my life, and a few of their stories are captured in this book, but there is one in particular who comes to mind that I want to tell you about. His name was Jim, and he was the general manager of the aerospace manufacturing plant where I worked early in my career.

At the time, I was working for McDonnell Douglas Corporation, one of the largest aerospace companies in the world, which was undergoing a significant transformation. In a quest to turn around chronic poor performance, our CEO decided to move forward with the implementation of a first-of-its-kind in the aerospace industry: an untraditional team-based approach to manufacturing based upon the Japanese labor concept of Total Quality Management (TQM) with elements of Lean manufacturing mixed in. The company leased the U.S. Air Force facility in my hometown of Columbus, Ohio, as the greenfield site, where they would build

– 1 –

sub-assemblies for the U.S. Air Force's new C-17 cargo plane, and they would do so under this new management philosophy—one of the first aerospace companies in the U.S. to do so. We would be affectionately referred to as Team Columbus.

At Team Columbus, I witnessed this transformation firsthand when nearly seventeen hundred of my fellow team members and I were introduced to a new management concept unlike anything we had been accustomed to. Instead of the traditional labor–management strife and conflict, with plenty of finger pointing and animosity, we would adopt a team-based culture that embraced a labor–management partnership. This approach empowered line workers to have significant input into problem-solving, decision-making, and other continuous improvement efforts.

This all sounded great, but I knew the culture of our workforce. I was steeped in it, and it would be a long climb to reach a point where there was enough trust and respect between management and the union to support this effort as a true partnership. To accomplish this, the company made a significant investment of time and money to hire the right people, and to train and develop the workforce in how to operate and succeed with this new approach. More importantly, it hired the right leader.

Jim was a new breed of executive manager, and it quickly became apparent why. He was strikingly different from any other manager I had encountered in my career. He had an uncanny ability to connect quickly with employees on a personal level through his honesty, authenticity, and dry sense of humor, while commanding authentic authority with his intelligence and credibility. More than a highly effective manager, he was a *leader* people were willing to follow, capable of garnering hard-won trust and respect from every team member, salaried and bargaining unit employees alike. Yet what really made him so influential was his ability to bring out the best in myself and many of my teammates, and he did so by sharing and living by two primary principles.

Jim the GM's Principle #1: You Are My First Priority

"Each of you is my number one priority. It's not the customer, the shareholders, or even my boss. All of these are important to making this plant a success, but they all fall in line behind you. Suppose we (the leadership team) do *our* job, providing you with the knowledge, tools, and resources you need to do your job, to learn and develop new skills and abilities, and create an environment where you are not only trusted but expected to make decisions regarding how the work gets done. I trust that all these other concerns will be satisfied."

These were inspiring words but more than just words with Jim. He not only talked the talk but walked the walk. He embraced diversity and inclusion long before it was a thing. He made us all feel like we belonged, that we were an essential part of our bigger team, regardless of our role or position, background, preferences, etc. No single individual was more or less important to the team. It was just as common to see him in his business suit as it was to see him with his tie tucked into his pocket and sleeves rolled up, strolling the shop floor or stopping by our morning production meetings to share a coffee with the team, or simply stopping by to say hello and ask how the family was doing. He displayed a seemingly natural ability and a personal desire to relate to others regardless of who they were. Anyone who spent any time with Jim soon realized that he cared about them as a person first and foremost, and the work was something that we were all engaged in together.

He also enabled us by providing us with the knowledge, skills, and tools we needed to do our job well, and for good reason. Jim constantly challenged us, individually and as teams, raising the bar of expectations to solve problems and make decisions. He was focused on continuously improving our performance while providing the coaching we needed to do so.

Lastly, Jim was all about celebrating our contributions whether we succeeded in reaching our goals or fell short. He valued our experience, but what he valued most were the lessons we were learning, and he expected us to apply them going forward.

Jim the GM's Principle #2: I Need All of You to Be Leaders

Secondly, Jim stressed that every single one of us had the potential to be an effective leader, regardless of our position or role on the team.

"We need all of you to develop the leader within you because at some point in time, perhaps today, tomorrow, this week, a leadership void will open up somewhere near to you: a problem to be solved, a decision to be made, an opportunity to make an improvement or to help one of your team members succeed. When it does, there may not be a manager or supervisor available, and we will need someone to step up, lean in, and take the lead to get the job done."

This was an entirely new concept for me to grasp, but the more I thought about it, the more I began to understand, embrace, and live it. With this new awareness, I began to observe and appreciate what leadership truly was and was not. All one had to do was look around and observe the dynamics of organizational life every day. Yes, there were managers, and there were subordinates, but it was obvious that not all managers were leaders, and not all leaders were managers. However, Jim knew there was one thing that everyone could share: the mindset of a servant leader. By bringing your best and helping others succeed, everyone reaches higher levels of success.

This mindset that Jim instilled was supported by a progressive learning and organizational development program. To begin with, all potential new hires, regardless of their position, were required to complete a behavioral assessment to ensure they demonstrated the expected team behaviors before joining Team Columbus. Additionally, once hired, all team members were required to complete a three-week training program called Discovery. Part orientation and part indoctrination, in Discovery we learned the importance of creating a culture of leadership, teamwork, empowerment, and continuous improvement to execute our TQM system effectively.

This was my first leadership development experience, and I loved it. As a front-line assembly mechanic, I was accustomed to the routine of drilling holes and filling them with rivets. While I enjoyed my work, I always knew I had more to contribute in terms of leadership and intellect. This life-changing experience opened a whole new world for my teammates and I, providing an opportunity to contribute our talents in ways we had never imagined possible.

With his simple yet highly effective leadership style, based entirely on two easy principles, Jim was successful at gaining amazing followership. Why? Because he was "one of us," down-to-earth, approachable, sometimes vulnerable, honest, and hard-working: He was just coming to work every day to give his best and to give his best to his team. He was the kind of person who lifted everyone he came in contact with to higher levels of personal performance. It was truly an extraordinary experience for me to observe.

Under Jim's leadership and in the culture he worked to create, I watched a workforce transform. Our operational performance soared, and in just two short years, Team Columbus became one of the highest-performing plants in the entire company. Soon, our plant was gaining work at the expense of our sister plants simply due to our capability for getting the job done.

We were proud. We were accomplished. We were world-class. Even more remarkable, however, was the transformation that occurred on a personal level for myself and many of my fellow team members. This servant leadership mindset and focus on personal growth not only improved operational performance but also had a profoundly positive impact on how we felt about the place we worked, how we felt and what we believed about ourselves, the people we worked with, how we interacted with each other and perhaps most important, how we lived our lives away from work.

I began to apply many of the leadership lessons and practices I was learning at work in my personal life. This began with *self-leadership* and the realization that you must first learn to lead yourself before you can ever lead others. I took this to heart, committing to my own self-awareness and personal development. This helped me gain more confidence in myself and improve my self-esteem, which in turn enhanced my relationships with those most important to me, helping me become a better husband, father, son, brother, and friend. Likewise, I held myself accountable by returning to school to complete my bachelor's degree. I was just one example. Many of my fellow coworkers shared the same sentiment, proving that the positive impact of Elevated Leadership extends far beyond the workplace.

This experience was a case study in servant leadership and employee engagement, some ten or twenty years before either would become part of the ongoing conversation. Over the years since, research has validated what my teammates and I at Team Columbus experienced firsthand due to Jim's leadership.

Although a small, isolated case study that may be lost in time, Jim's leadership was transformational, turning a crusty, unionized, rough-and-tumble, average-performing workforce into Team Columbus, a world-class manufacturing facility. While doing so, he made a powerful positive impression on many who would carry it with them for the rest of their lives.

Team Columbus, as it came to be known, was simply a much nicer place to work than it ever was before Jim arrived. The entire experience and the chance to witness such effective leadership was an eye-opener for me—so much so that I chose to make a career of helping leaders, their teams, and organizations be more successful. I have watched with humble appreciation and have learned from other leadership gurus who approached leadership in this way, such as Robert Greenleaf, who first introduced the servant leadership model, James McGregor Burns, whose book *Leadership* introduced the field of leadership studies and developed the Transformational Leadership theory, and others like Peter Drucker, Tom Peters, Ken Blanchard, John Maxwell, and Simon Sinek, to name just a few of my favorites.

In all my years since, I have followed the lessons of these extraordinary thought leaders and continued to practice the two simple principles I learned from Jim the GM:

1. Make those you lead your highest business priority. If you focus on developing and enabling those you lead, all other stakeholders, including yourself, stand a much better chance of achieving success.
2. Develop leadership potential in everyone. Leadership is a mindset and a heartset that can be shared by all. Anyone can develop their leadership abilities and, in turn, raise the performance of those around them.

Having taught, coached, and interacted with well over fifteen hundred leaders during my career, I can tell you that if you choose to be a leader, you must adopt a servant-leader mindset and focus on developing the same in others as you lead them to ever-higher levels of personal and organizational success. That is the only way an organization can possibly prevent and fill the leadership voids that might occur in yourself, your team, and your organization.

CHAPTER TWO

Birth of E3C3

In the summer of 2013, our executive leadership team tasked me with assisting our global director of operational excellence in designing, developing, and implementing our company-wide Business Excellence System (BES). This system provided a structured framework for continuous improvement and learning, requiring a thorough organizational assessment across seven core areas of performance excellence: Leadership, Customers, Measurement, Analysis and Knowledge Management, Workforce, Operations, and Results. The results of these assessments were benchmarked against recognized standards of excellence, offering valuable feedback on strengths and areas for improvement. Each facility or location was then expected to act on these insights to enhance operational performance. The success of the BES—and the benefits it delivered—relied entirely on the unwavering support of leadership and the full engagement of the entire workforce.

We started working together, and within three months, we launched the initiative at our first three business units, including our largest facility in western Pennsylvania. We ran an intensive communication campaign, and within six weeks we conducted the first round of BES implementation which involved leadership and team BES training in support of the effort. The progress was slow for the first few months. Still, after a year of implementing the BES system, we showed impressive results across the board. As we slowly expanded implementation, we met several pockets of resistance and slow adoption. After a year, it became clear that our progress had stalled due to the lack of leadership commitment and accountability in various pockets of the organization. As a result, we started to fall short of our implementation goals over the next three months. At this point, the only way to fill this void and sustain the incredible momentum we had achieved was for the executive leadership team to hold themselves and other key leaders accountable for keeping the commitments that were made. Unfortunately, that simply did not happen.

Two weeks before our second annual BES conference, I received a phone call from our global director of operational excellence sharing the news that our new CEO and keynote speaker for the event would not be attending the conference. Furthermore, he had ordered all future implementation activities to be halted beginning immediately. I was stunned. After a year and a half of incredible progress, impressive operational improvements and active engagement from 68% of the workforce, the project ended. All activity ceased and team was disbanded.

It was a bitter pill to swallow, and I am sure there was a logical, business reason for taking such a measure; however, I will never know why. We were not privy to that information, and no further explanation was given. All I know is this was a difficult time for the team and all those across the company who had bought into what we were doing and had been putting so much work into the implementation. We had stumbled across and were sucked into a large leadership void.

I have seen the great, the good, the bad, and the ugly when it comes to organizational leadership, and this was just the latest example of a leadership void. Whenever I see something like this occur, I am reminded of the words from Jim, my former general manager, "Beware of the leadership voids and be prepared to fill them before they do any further harm." It was too late in this case.

Not long after all this went down, frustrated by the turn of events, I was lying awake one warm summer evening. I knew at this stage of my career, change happens, and we have to learn to manage it, to remain resilient and work through it. Nonetheless, I was continuing to ask why, staring up at the ceiling asking God and his universe. Why do things like this happen so frequently? Why, so many times, do we find ourselves lacking effective leadership when it is needed most?

That led to my next few questions. What would my most admired leaders have done (or not done) in this situation like this? I went to a deeper level. What was it that set these leaders apart from others? What enabled them to lead others, and lead other leaders, to higher levels of success while others often fell short, leaving us needing more?

The answer, which I really wasn't expecting, returned to me like a tsunami wave, with perfect clarity, brevity, practicality, and common sense. Six words: **Embrace, Empower, Engage, Challenge, Coach, and Celebrate.** That was it. The answer. It's as simple as that, three Es and three Cs.

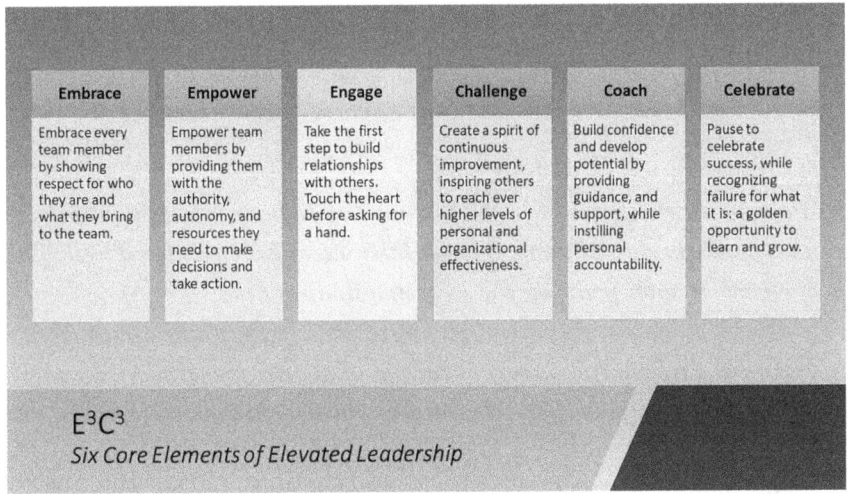

The Six Core Elements

Oh, and it gets even better. The message continued. As I pondered these six things, I reflected on my experiences and memories of the most impactful leaders I had encountered. These leaders seamlessly incorporated these principles into everything they did; it was how they led. Sure, it was about their character, their knowledge, their skill, and their actions, but it was deeper than that—something primal, something elemental about leadership.

Unable to sleep, I got out of bed and stepped into my office. For the next thirty minutes, I made notes of what I had just experienced. The seed for E3C3 Leadership was firmly planted in my mind, where it would germinate for a couple of years. I believed I was onto something inherently good, important, and beautiful in its simplicity—something uniquely valuable to share with the world. All I needed was a golden thread to weave it all together. A couple of years later, an incredible personal adventure up on a mountain would provide that thread.

CHAPTER THREE

Rainier

"Perhaps the greatest value of all that we receive from 'The Mountain' is that of renewed inspiration. The soul that does not respond to a feeling of reverence upon gazing at the great mountain is dead. 'The Mountain That Was God'—Even the Indians sensed its great power, its air of mystery, the feeling of mighty forces and of majesty it engenders in the human soul. And so they imbued it with supernatural powers."

Mount Rainier Nature Notes, Charles Landis, Ranger, Naturalist, 1931

I have a confession to make. Some years ago, I became infatuated with a mountain and eventually engaged in a lofty love affair. Yes, that's right, a mountain. But wait, don't judge, let me explain that this is no ordinary mountain. The Native Americans who settled in this part of Washington State called it *Tahoma*, "the mother of all waters," and, I believe, rightly so. We know it today as Mt. Rainier, and this is the story about how this love affair inspired me to write this book.

My first Rainier encounter came just two years after my wife and I wed. It was our first trip to visit my new in-laws, who happened to live in Tacoma, Washington. When I arrived at the airport, I was eager to see this iconic landmark of the Great Northwest. Unfortunately, the first three days were cloudy and overcast in true Northwest Washington fashion, so she remained "hidden under her blankets," as the locals say. Finally, on the morning of the fourth day of our visit, the weather changed, and we were greeted by a clear, sunny morning. As I strode downstairs to grab a cup of coffee, my new mother-in-law met me at the bottom of the steps, and although she could not speak much English, she knew what I had been waiting for. She smiled and motioned for me to enter the kitchen, then pointed out the window above the sink.

Nowhere to be seen for three days, the mountain was there now, perfectly framed by the window. I was awestruck by what I saw; she stood on the horizon, glistening in the sun with a clear-blue sky as a background. Streams of steam emanating from the summit turned to clouds and trailed off to the north. What struck me was how large she appeared—some 65 miles from Tacoma, Mt. Rainier utterly dominated the landscape. This was love at first sight, where and when my love affair with Mt. Rainier all started. From that moment on, I felt as if that mountain was calling me, inviting me to get closer and get to know her better.

Unfortunately, a well-intentioned trip to Rainier National Park the following morning was cut short. While the sun was shining from Tacoma to Ashford just outside the park entrance, no sooner had we reached Paradise Inn had the sky begun to turn an ominous blue-gray. In a matter of minutes, several park ranger cars pulled into the parking lot with flashers on, the rangers started rounding up the motorists to pack up and return down the mountain ahead of the bad weather that was rolling in. So much for my closer encounter! We scurried down Paradise Valley Parkway and returned to Tacoma under a clear blue sky. Gazing back, we could see that she was covered in a thick, angry-looking dark cloud, looking more like Mordor than Mt. Rainier. The following day, we heard on the news that four feet of snow had fallen overnight at Paradise Inn, and it was still snowing. Wintertime had come to Mt. Rainier. Nonetheless, what was initially a curiosity for a guy who loved the mountains had become somewhat of an obsession. I vowed to return as soon as possible.

That time came nine years later while traveling for business in Chehalis, Washington. After having finished up with work a little early on a Tuesday afternoon, our boss declared the day complete, giving us some extra time to enjoy the beautiful, late summer afternoon and evening. I knew exactly what I was going to do with my free time. I decided to take a trip out to Paradise Inn at Mt. Rainier and hike. The way I had it figured, a beautiful two-hour trip out, a one hour hike, and then two hours back to my hotel in Chehalis.

I left the hotel at 4:30 p.m. The weather was spectacular as I made my way east toward Rainier. As I made my way through the mountains, weaving in and out of the deep, thickly forested valleys, I would occasionally capture a glimpse of her—each time from a slightly different angle and growing more prominent on the horizon. Eventually, I arrived in Ashford and the southwestern entrance to Mt. Rainier National Park. As I cruised under the entranceway, I thanked God that I was finally back, still trying to get closer to the mountain.

After another twenty minutes winding my way up Paradise Valley Road, I finally arrived again at Paradise Inn, that stunning, early twentieth century building rich in alpine architecture constructed entirely from the enormous logs of native Douglas fir trees. The lodge sat at 5,400 ft. above sea level and was the highest point anyone could get to in an automobile. For those who wanted to go higher, it would have to be on foot; that is precisely what I planned to do.

I arrived at exactly 6:40 p.m. I set the timer on my watch for 20 minutes. I would hike for twenty minutes, take a ten-minute break, and return to my car in time to make it back to the hotel before it was too late. Fortunately, it was early July, and there was not a cloud in the sky. I would have the advantage of a late sunset. With my timer running, I started up the Skyline Trail Loop. This popular trail winds itself around the alpine pastures above Paradise Inn. At every turn, I took the one that led uphill. I was interested in gaining a great view of the mountain and the valley below from the highest vantage point possible within my twenty-minute time frame. After about ten minutes, as the pavement ended, I noticed fewer and fewer casual hikers along the trail. The trail became substantially more challenging with steeper elevation gains. I paused every hundred feet or so to take in the sights, sounds, smells, and natural ambiance that surrounded me. A real sensual overload.

I continued another few minutes before my alarm went off, telling me I was at the end of my trail for the night, so I looked around. I didn't take long to find a good-sized boulder to use as a bench, so I took a seat to relax and drink it all in. There I sat in silence, contemplating life and meditating on the beauty of God's creation. I gazed down and out across Paradise Valley, the lodge already far off below. My eyes followed the path of the Nisqually River, making its way down the valley and then onto

Puget Sound. Upwards, I lifted my gaze to the lofty and jagged peaks of the neighboring mountains. Then, finally, ever upwards to her summit, still glistening with an orange glow as the sun tilted to the western sky.

Then I looked down again to see a tiny seedling making its way up through the melting snow. I thought to myself, *From the grand and glorious to the meek and humble, His creation is once astounding and sublime.* In the distance, I heard deep, ominous cracking and knocking coming from deep down inside the glaciers. Then I felt the wind pick up just a bit, with a few stronger gusts whispering through the alpine forest. I listened. Then I heard it.

"Your journey, no matter where you have been or what you have endured so far, is not over. The next chapter starts here."

Some might say I was talking to myself, caught up in personal affirmation, but I know otherwise. There was a reason I was there, in that spot, at that time. It had been a totally unplanned and impromptu trip, yet there I was, and this was a message that I didn't expect to hear. Nonetheless, I didn't question it. In my mind, God was speaking to me through his miracle of creation. I looked down at my watch. It was time to go, so I bid farewell to my resting place and started descending the mountain, retracing my route.

Not long after I reached the point where the trail was paved once again, I saw a group of what appeared to be a hearty bunch of climbers coming down from much higher climbs. As we came together, I said hello to everyone and joined their party for the remainder of my hike.

I turned to the gentleman closest to me. "So, I am guessing this bunch has been doing climbing."

He nodded. "Yep, you'd be guessing right."

"Ahh, I see, interesting. That's got to be quite a trip," I replied, somewhat in awe and now extremely curious.

A young lady behind us spoke up. "It's incredible!" she said with great enthusiasm, even though she looked thoroughly exhausted, as did all of them. Then she added, "You should go sometime."

I glanced at her briefly and smiled, then looked back up to the summit.

I returned my gaze to her, grinned, and said, "I just might have to do that."

They all smiled and nodded their heads, as another gentleman added, "If you're up for a challenge, this could be it."

I gave him a nod and a smile, too. "I'll keep that in mind."

Just a few hundred more paces and I arrived with my newfound group of mountaineering friends at the Paradise Inn parking area. I headed toward my car as the climbing party turned to their bus.

When I reached my car, it was 6:45 p.m. It was time to head back down the mountain and on back to Chehalis, concluding what was, to this day, the best after-work walk I've ever had. I felt fully refreshed and quite mesmerized by what I had experienced in such a short period of time there on that mountain.

As I made my way back to the hotel all I could think of were those mystical moments that captured my fancy and left me with more than a few profound messages. Without a doubt, I was left with a mission in my mind and in my heart. My purpose was clear. I knew I had a mountain to climb, both literally and figuratively. That day, I added the Mt. Rainier summit attempt to my bucket list and determined that someday I would make it happen.

Seventeen years later, in August 2015, I joined a group of like-minded individuals, led by an exceptional team of mountain guides, for a summit attempt of Mt. Rainier. I've shared many reflections from this journey in the following pages, and for good reason.

It was this mountain challenge that helped me bring to light the idea of *E3C3: The Six Core Elements of Elevated Leadership*. Finally, I had that golden thread that I needed to tie this all together, and the inspiration for E3C3. During this attempt, I saw firsthand how these Six Core Elements could be put into practice thanks to the efforts of the climbing part and the mountain guides. There were obvious parallels between the leadership and teamwork shown on the mountain and what was possible in an organization.

You, your team, and your organization have both personal and shared goals. Think of it as the summit of your success, whatever that might look like for you. What are you trying to accomplish? How will the team reach its goal and ensure that everyone returns home safely? On the trip, your team is undoubtedly going to encounter obstacles, problems and other types of challenges, and it will take a team of leaders to overcome them. I invite you to think of E3C3 as your team guidebook. It includes a proven route plan to guide you to the summit and a methodology that ensures everyone on the team achieves success, whether you are leading yourself, leading others, or leading other leaders. By following this guidebook anyone can become an Elevated Leader.

First, think about it from the perspective of leading yourself: Self-leadership is about seeking out new stretch goals that push you beyond your comfort zone. It is the most effective form of personal development. It involves holding yourself accountable for your actions and remaining committed to continuous improvement. It also requires the self-awareness and vulnerability to admit that you cannot succeed alone, recognizing that others' success or failure will also depend on you.

Next, consider it from the perspective of leading others: Even a rookie climber soon realizes that mountaineering is a team sport like no other. The moment you clip yourself onto the rope with your team, you are there to stay, and the success of every individual becomes intertwined with the success of the team. To reach the summit or goal, a team of leaders is essential, because at any moment, the team's success may rely on your leadership ability.

Lastly, view this analogy from the perspective of leading other leaders: I say hail to the mighty mountain guides! These impressive leaders guide their climbing teams up the mountain toward a shared goal. They lead others to higher levels of success, by making others their priority and while developing leadership capabilities. They exemplify a balanced approach toward performance, one moment focused entirely on the technical nature of the climb, then shifting to human nature with ease as needed, providing just the right amount of support and direction for those they lead.

CHAPTER FOUR

Beware the Leadership Void

Undoubtedly, we've all experienced situations where the absence of effective leadership has led to uncomfortable and difficult moments in our personal and professional lives. When progress appears to halt, it's often due to a leadership void that requires filling. These gaps may start small, affecting individuals or teams and causing temporary setbacks and minor frustrations. However, if these voids are left unattended, they can escalate, leading to significant issues and failures across the entire organization. It's crucial to address these leadership voids promptly, wherever and whenever they emerge. Rather than resorting to blame or termination, Elevated Leaders guide and nurture their teams, assisting them in filling the void and achieving their objectives.

Leadership, a concept that has been a part of human civilization for thousands of years, has a rich and evolving history. Modern leadership theory began in the late nineteenth century with what scholars call the Great Man Period (1840s–1900s), a time when it was believed that great leaders were born, not made, and only a select few individuals possessed the natural ability to lead. However, leadership theory evolved with the introduction of Trait Theory in the early twentieth century (1910s–1940s), which posited that leadership was more about traits and characteristics that distinguished leaders from non-leaders.

From traits and characteristics, the focus shifted to observable behaviors in the mid-twentieth century. Behavioral Theory (1940s–1950s) suggested that leadership could be learned and developed by adopting and demonstrating specific behaviors. Then, with the introduction of Contingency Theory in the 1960s, Fred Fiedler proposed that the effectiveness of a leader's style depended on the situation and the relationship between the leader and their followers.

Leadership theory, once confined to academia, began to gain mainstream attention in the early-to-mid 1980s with the emergence of the Cultural and Transformational Era. This era began with Transformational Leadership Theory (1970s–1980s), which proposed that a leader's ability to inspire and motivate their followers could achieve extraordinary results. Soon after, the groundbreaking Situational Leadership theory (late 1970s–1980s) was introduced by Ken Blanchard and Paul Hersey, contending that leaders should adapt and flex their style based on the needs of their followers.

This transformational period also shed light on the growing appreciation for leadership and its importance over management. Leadership was recognized as a set of skills and behaviors that anyone could learn and develop. It became clear that leadership was about inspiring, motivating, and helping others achieve extraordinary results, and about having the ability to flex one's style to meet the needs of others. The fact was made plain: Not all managers are leaders, and more importantly, not all leaders are necessarily managers. This change in thinking was propelled by high-profile business consultants, celebrated business gurus, and renowned scholars who transformed the study of leadership into a thriving industry and a prominent topic of discussion in the business world. This appreciation for leadership had entered mainstream thinking.

By the mid-to-late 1990s, global economic factors and the tech revolution put immense pressure on business organizations to become more agile and responsive to constant change. During this time, the need for effective leadership became more important than ever as workers began to prefer being "led" over being "managed," and in many cases, that need went unmet. This was the origin of the leadership void, and it remains in place in many ways, even today.

A Great Betrayal

This crucial distinction between management and leadership became increasingly evident in the world of big business during the 1980s and early 1990s. In 1975, Mr. John L. Neuman of McKinsey and Company introduced the concept of Overhead Value Analysis, leading to an era of downsizing, rightsizing, and reorganizing in companies. These measures were taken to increase competitiveness, market share, and ultimately drive-up stock prices. However, the flattening of organizational structures resulted in the loss of thousands of jobs. Up to this point, cost-cutting layoffs had primarily impacted front-line workers, fueling the growth of labor unions for decades. This time it was different. These efforts cut a much wider swath through the entire organization, including middle, senior, and executive management, and other key salaried personnel.

While Neuman argued that these measures were "necessary to maintain the financial and operational health of the organization," they failed to consider the human element, which is a fundamental component of operational health. The shortsighted focus on financial and operational performance metrics ignored the importance of the longer view and the human side of the organization.

For those who delved deeper beyond the surface level, it was unequivocally clear that these management efforts were causing irreparable harm to the organization, specifically to the relationship between C-suite managers and their employees. The failure to comprehend or appreciate the human element of the organization and the distinction between management and leadership resulted in a significant betrayal. As a result, some of the most important characteristics of a healthy organization were lost, and we have been trying to get them back ever since. Trust was the first casualty, followed by respect, with loyalty not far behind. The impact on employee engagement was profound, even if we weren't measuring it at the time. Today, it's evident we are still feeling the repercussions of this catastrophic leadership void in our teams and organizations.

By the mid-1980s, the digital revolution was transforming the workplace, redefining the type of work performed, and the knowledge and skills required. As a result, the new front-line worker quickly became highly valued for their unique knowledge and technical skills, surpassing traditional manual labor. The era of the knowledge worker had begun, and the balance of power was shifting in favor of the employee. By 2000, the impact on workplace culture was evident. Employees were tired of old management practices and the culture of command-and-control leadership.

In the years since, with each generation, our understanding and the way we look at leadership has continued to evolve and build on the last. Likewise, our expectations of our workplaces have continued to evolve as well, More simply put, leadership is wanted and needed. We know what to look for, when it is needed, and we know when it is lacking. As a result, leadership voids are occurring at a rapid rate all around us. In order to fill these voids, a new way of thinking about leadership is required.

In an article by Sihame Benmira and Moyosolu Agboola titled "Evolution of Leadership Theory" for the *BMJ Leader* (2021), the authors describe how leadership theory has been changing.

> *"Focusing on one aspect or dimension of leadership cannot address all the complexity of the phenomenon. As the world becomes more complex and challenging, the need for leadership theories that support circumstances of rapid change, disruptive technological innovation, and increasing globalization emerged. This led to a new leadership era that moves away from traditional theories of leadership, which define leadership as a unidirectional, top-down influencing process, drawing a distinct line between leaders and followers. Instead, the focus is on the complex interactions among the leader, the followers, the situation, and the system as a whole, with particular attention dedicated to the latent leadership capacities of everyone in the organization."*

This way of thinking about leadership lies at the heart of Elevated Leadership. No one leader, or select group of leaders, will ever have the capacity to identify, prevent, or fill all the leadership voids that occur. It takes a team of leaders, everyone with a role to play, and it begins by identifying those leadership voids and accounting for their impact. These leadership voids occur in ourselves, our teams, and our organizations.

Leadership Voids on a Personal Level (When Leading Yourself)

When we think of leadership, we often focus on leading others, which is understandable. However, we tend to overlook perhaps the most important form of leadership: the ability to lead ourselves first. Self-leadership is fundamental and foundational to all other forms of leadership. It's important to note that not all leaders are managers; in fact, most leaders are not. This distinction is crucial in the context of Elevated Leadership and the application of the Six Core Elements.

Unfortunately, many of us view leadership as a role reserved for those in designated positions of authority. This mindset limits our concept of leadership and hinders our ability to reach our full leadership potential, both personally and organizationally. Addressing personal leadership voids requires a broader understanding of leadership that begins with self-leadership.

When identifying and addressing our personal leadership voids, it is important to consider the impact they have on our individual effectiveness and our ability to contribute to team success. The following are some symptoms of personal leadership voids that can occur when we fail to demonstrate the Six Core Elements on a regular basis:

- *Decreased Self-Awareness:* Without embracing your strengths and weaknesses, you miss opportunities for growth and self-improvement.
- *Lack of Progress:* Avoiding responsibility and failing to empower yourself results in stagnation and unfulfilled potential.
- *Reduced Motivation:* Inconsistency and a lack of focus lead to unfinished projects and a sense of inefficacy.
- *Limited Growth:* Avoiding challenges prevents you from developing resilience and adaptability.
- *Stifled Development:* Resistance to feedback and self-coaching hinders your ability to learn and evolve.
- *Burnout and Dissatisfaction:* Failing to celebrate achievements leads to burnout and a lack of fulfillment.

All leadership voids begin on a personal level. By recognizing and addressing these leadership voids, you can improve your self-leadership and personal effectiveness, while enhancing personal well-being. Leading ourselves requires honesty, humility, vulnerability, and a commitment to personal development. Elevated leaders admit they don't have all the answers and ideas, and they need others to succeed. They are aware of their strengths, preferences, biases, and shortcomings and are open to receiving feedback from others.

Awareness is one thing; taking action to increase personal effectiveness is another. Elevated leaders hold themselves and others accountable for ongoing personal learning and development. They understand the importance of equipping themselves with whatever it takes to fill any leadership voids they may have. Likewise, the team and the organization must recognize and value the concept of self-leadership and commit to developing the leadership potential of every team member.

Leadership Voids at the Team Level (When Leading Others)

"Leadership is a team sport." —Simon Sinek

The concept of teamwork has significantly evolved over the past thirty years, transforming from traditional, functional organizations to complex, matrixed, value-driven, cross-functional teams. Nowadays, much of an organization's success depends heavily on effective teamwork, with countless organizations of all sizes relying on it to achieve their goals. However, not all teams are created equal; they vary in developmental maturity and rely on each member's leadership abilities to lead others effectively. When these leadership needs go unmet, team leadership voids emerge, impacting team effectiveness. Below are examples of such voids and their consequences.

Impact on Team Effectiveness

- *Decreased Inclusivity:* Failing to value team diversity results in missed opportunities for innovative solutions and reduces the team's overall effectiveness.
- *Disempowerment:* Micromanagement and failure to delegate hinder team members' ability to take ownership and initiative, leading to disengagement and low morale.
- *Poor Collaboration:* Ineffective communication and lack of engagement result in misunderstandings, errors, and a lack of cohesion within the team.

- *Stunted Growth:* Avoiding challenges and setting low expectations prevent team members from developing new skills and achieving their full potential.
- *Limited Development:* Lack of coaching and mentorship stifles professional growth and reduces the overall competency of the team.
- *Decreased Motivation:* Failing to celebrate achievements leads to a lack of motivation and can contribute to burnout among team members.

All these issues are evidence of leadership voids at the team level. When these voids occur, they have a direct and negative impact on performance and can lead to stress, anxiety, animosity, and fear, negatively impacting the team's well-being. By recognizing and addressing these leadership voids, all leaders, regardless of their role, can enhance their effectiveness in guiding and inspiring their teams, fostering a supportive and high-performing environment.

Leadership Voids at the Organizational Level (Leading Other Leaders)

The shift towards a flat, team-based organizational culture has rendered obsolete the old, functional, command-and-control approach to leadership. Shared leadership, focusing on teamwork, inclusion, collaboration, engagement, accountability, and ongoing development significantly increases an organization's leadership capacity. Today, managing people is insufficient; it is leadership, especially Elevated Leadership, which can propel you and your team to unprecedented heights. Adopting this philosophy when leading other leaders can help your organization reach its full potential and ensure long-term success.

Leadership voids at the organizational level often stem from personal leadership voids at the highest levels. When unaddressed, these voids grow, affecting the entire team and organization. Below are some examples of leadership voids that can occur when leading other leaders.

Impact on Organizational Effectiveness

- *Reduced Innovation and Creativity:* Missing out on diverse perspectives and innovative ideas due to a failure to value leadership diversity stifles the organization's ability to develop creative solutions and adapt to changing environments.
- *Decreased Employee Morale and Engagement:* A lack of empowerment, recognition, and effective communication demotivates leaders and their teams, leading to overall low morale and engagement throughout the organization.
- *Stifled Leadership Development and Succession Planning:* Without mentorship, coaching, and challenging opportunities, emerging leaders fail to develop, resulting in a weak leadership pipeline and potential future leadership crises.
- *Increased Turnover Rates:* Frustration from centralized decision-making and poor communication drives talented leaders to leave the organization, leading to higher turnover rates and the associated costs of recruitment and training.
- *Negative Organizational Culture:* Leadership voids create a negative organizational culture where innovation, recognition, and growth are stifled, making it challenging to attract and retain top talent and reducing overall organizational effectiveness.

Regardless of where and when leadership voids occur at the organizational level, they can prevent individuals and teams from achieving the success they deserve. The costs to the organization are numerous, including decreased engagement, reduced sales, lack of innovation, lost productivity, poor quality, increased safety incident rates, and high turnover rates. The impact of leadership voids at an organizational level extends beyond business performance, and these voids can negatively affect the personal well-being of all employees, which is perhaps the most damaging of all. By recognizing and addressing these leadership voids, senior leaders can lead other leaders more effectively, fostering a supportive and high-performing organizational environment.

PART TWO
ASCENT

CHAPTER FIVE

Filling the Leadership Voids

It is clear that no single leader or select group of leaders can fill all the leadership voids that inevitably arise. Expecting such a feat is not only unrealistic but impossible. Addressing these voids requires a collective effort—a team of leaders, an organization of leaders—each playing a crucial role when and where leadership is needed. This principle is central to the E3C3 methodology driving the need for an inclusive, collective approach to leadership development that ensures everyone in the organization has a role to play in creating and Elevated Leadership culture.

The Case for E3C3

What must Elevated Leaders know, say, and do, regardless of their role or position? The solution is simple yet profound. Traditionally, organizations have addressed these questions by identifying and defining core leadership competencies and creating leadership competency models. As I explored E3C3 more deeply, its simplicity struck me. I questioned whether this revelation could withstand rigorous academic scrutiny. How would it compare to the multitude of existing leadership models? In my humble, honest opinion, there was little I could add to the remarkable academic work that had already inspired E3C3.

However, after further reflection and discussions with trusted colleagues, I realized that comparison was unnecessary. E3C3 and the Six Core Elements represent more than a model—they embody a methodology that requires a shared mindset and heartset. E3C3 serves as the organizational foundation upon which all leadership, learning, and development efforts should be built.

A Word on Competencies

Specific skills, behaviors, and attributes are essential for effective leadership. These competencies enable leaders to inspire, guide, and influence others to achieve organizational goals and create a positive work environment. However, relying solely on leadership competency models often falls short in driving the desired organizational behavior changes. While competencies are crucial, they lack impact without a foundational leadership culture to support them. In the realm of Elevated Leadership, culture comes first.

Moreover, leadership competency models frequently fail due to their complexity and ambiguity, making them difficult to scale effectively across an organization. This is where E3C3, with its Six Core Elements of Elevated Leadership, becomes particularly relevant. E3C3 serves as both a methodology and a model that is practical, straightforward, and aligned with the real-world needs of organizations.

The Power of E3C3 Leadership

E3C3 Leadership focuses first on creating a culture conducive to leadership development—a foundation upon which all efforts should be built. Unfortunately, the importance of this foundational culture is often overlooked, misunderstood, or inadequately established. The strength of E3C3 lies in its simplicity, practicality, scalability, and impact. E3C3 is easy to understand and relate to, making it accessible to anyone with the right mindset and heartset. It offers practical, actionable steps that individuals can take to elevate themselves and their teams. This simplicity makes E3C3 highly scalable and inclusive as it is shared and embedded within teams and organizations.

As a leadership model, it's important to understand that the Six Core Elements are fundamental. Just as primary colors create the entire spectrum of the rainbow, these Six Core Elements are foundational to all other leadership competencies. By first embedding E3C3 into leadership development efforts, organizations can build a robust and practical foundation for further growth, with specific competencies supported and aligned with these Six Core Elements. Most importantly, by focusing on and demonstrating the Six Core Elements together, individuals and teams will experience measurable improvements in performance, employee engagement, and overall well-being.

At this point, you may be asking, "What does this actually mean in practice?" This is a legitimate question that deserves a clear answer. First, it is important to define what these Six Core Elements are and what they mean. Chapter Twelve of this book goes into detail defining each of the elements and their supporting competencies, but beyond that, what might it look like when leaders put them into practice?

Perhaps the most compelling case for E3C3 is to share real-world examples of how Elevated Leaders I've known have modeled the Six Core Elements in diverse environments and from different perspectives. Tying these stories together is my ongoing reflection on climbing Mt. Rainier with my climbing team, led by mountain guides who also exemplified the Six Core Elements. The unexpected and invaluable lessons in leadership, teamwork, and personal growth that I learned from that adventure are both practical and applicable in our personal and organizational lives. It illustrates that anyone in any situation or setting that involves a team or group effort can enhance their leadership abilities and help drive others to higher levels of success with the Six Core Elements of Elevated Leadership.

CHAPTER SIX

Embrace

Embrace those you wish to lead and take action to ensure that people feel like they belong and are valued for who they are and what they bring to the table.

"People don't care how much you know until they know how much you care."

— John Maxwell

Embrace goes beyond mere acceptance; it involves actively recognizing and appreciating the unique strengths, perspectives, and contributions of each team member. Elevated Leaders understand that success is not just about achieving goals but about building a culture where everyone feels seen, heard, and valued. By fostering an environment of trust and mutual respect, they ensure that every individual is empowered to bring their full selves to work, contributing their best ideas and efforts to the collective success.

When employees perceive their workplace as inclusive, they are more likely to be engaged, motivated, and productive. A sense of belonging not only enhances individual satisfaction and performance but also strengthens the overall cohesion and effectiveness of the team. Conversely, a lack of inclusion can lead to feelings of isolation and disengagement, which can negatively impact morale, reduce productivity, and create challenges that disrupt organizational stability. That is why, in today's diverse and interconnected world, creating an inclusive workplace is more important than ever. Elevated Leaders prioritize initiatives that promote inclusivity, such as celebrating diversity, encouraging open dialogue, and providing equal opportunities for growth and development. They are committed to creating a culture where differences are not just tolerated but celebrated, recognizing that these differences are the source of innovation and resilience. Ultimately, embracing others is about building a community where every individual feels a deep sense of belonging and purpose.

Base Camp Orientation

When you join a team of mountaineers on a quest to reach the top of your mountain, you may not get to choose who those people might be. All you know is that you share one essential thing: the mindset and the heartset to reach the summit—and more importantly, to return safely. You must quickly learn to appreciate diversity and inclusion because you have no choice. You embrace the situation and the people climbing with you because when you all clip onto the same rope, you are responsible not only for your own safety but also for that of every team member. This was one of the most notable lessons I took away from my experience of climbing Mount Rainier. Regardless of the diversity, the strangeness, the unfamiliarity, and the different levels of skill and experience, there is safety to be found in the team, and in this case, your life may depend on it.

My adventure began two days before the actual climb. I arrived at Ashford Base Camp for the orientation session just before one in the afternoon. With butterflies in my stomach, I parked my car and made my way across the camp, eventually spotting a hand-drawn sign on poster board that read 'TEAM SEVEN BASE CAMP ORIENTATION' above one of the four shelter houses surrounding the office and equipment barn. As I approached, I was greeted by a young woman and two young men, likely in their early twenties, who were busy comparing notes on the clipboards they held. They paused their conversation just long enough to say hello.

"Hello!" they all said in unison.

One of the men stepped toward me with an outstretched hand. "My name is Gregg," he said. "I am the lead guide for our trip." Then he turned his attention to his colleagues. "This is Sonya," he explained.

She reached out and shook my hand. "Good to have you with us," she said.

Then Gregg turned to the other and added, "And this is KM, Kilimanjaro Master." He said this with a big grin on his face.

The other, slightly older man stepped over to shake my hand. "Only pay attention to him when he is serious," he said, smiling, with a noticeable Austrian German accent. "His jokes are really bad. Hi, my name is Klaus, Klaus Mühlbauerhofer, but everyone calls me KM."

Gregg then noticed that I was glancing at their clipboards and explained. "We were just going over notes. Feel free to take a seat and make yourself comfortable. I'm sure the others will be joining us soon." I nodded and took a seat at one of the picnic tables. Sure enough, no sooner had I sat down than several others began to join us. We all shook hands and introduced ourselves before taking our seats around the tables. Six of those in attendance joined Gregg, Sonya, and KM at one end of the shelter house: our eight mountain guides.

Gregg clapped his hands to get everyone's attention. "Hello! Hello, everyone! Time to get started," he shouted over the din of the conversations around the tables. In seconds, the place was quiet.

"Hi, I am Gregg, for those I have yet to meet. I will be your lead guide for our ascent up the mountain. I just want to first congratulate you on your decision to take on a challenge like this. Only a very small percentage of people in the world have summited a mountain, and even fewer have summited Mount Rainier, so welcome." He paused with arms outstretched and palms up.

"Now, from this point forward, it starts to get real."

When he said this, the butterflies in my belly took flight again.

He went on. "This afternoon is your orientation. First on our agenda is a movie. Yes, a movie," he said, as if reading our minds. "We're all going to gather in the camp lodge to watch a forty-minute video that will fully introduce you to what you are about to experience. We like to keep our teams fully informed and aware of what you might expect on the climb up Mount Rainier." He walked casually over to one of the tables and picked up a device in his hand, then continued, "After the video, if your hearts and minds are still set on reaching the summit, we will grab our packs and our gear, then meet back here where we will take inventory of all the necessary items and explain their uses." He held up the device he had in his hand. "Like my favorite, the avalanche beacon, if by chance you get buried under the snow." Gregg smiled but soon realized no one else was smiling.

KM leaned over to me and murmured, "See, I told you his jokes are bad."

Gregg heard KM but kept going, undaunted. "Seriously folks, I owe my life to this device. Four years ago, I was buried under eight feet of snow because of an avalanche that occurred while climbing in Colorado. I don't say this to scare you, but just to emphasize how important the Base Camp Orientation is. A large part of mountaineering is awareness: personal awareness, awareness of your surroundings, and awareness of each other." He paused briefly, then held up his hands. "But first, before we get into all of that, we are going to take some time to get better acquainted. So, let's make our way around the group here, each of you taking a few minutes to share whatever you would like. Within reason, of course. We are in a mixed crowd here." Gregg finally managed to get a laugh from the team. He continued, "So, your name, where you're from, your interests, your hobbies, pets—whatever you'd like to share. We want to know you better. However, be prepared to answer the most important question of all: Why? Why have you decided to take on this challenge?" He paused and looked around at our faces as we were already starting to contemplate his last question. "OK, then, what are you waiting for?"

For the next thirty minutes, we managed to get much better acquainted as we shared with each other some insight into our personal lives. There was Greta, a very young, but very experienced mountaineer from Belarus. There was Hitomi, a middle-aged, Japanese engineer from Virginia, here for his first climb. Alberto, a big, tall gentleman with a thick black beard was there with his younger and much smaller and brother Jesus from Venezuela. They were just here for their next adventure, filming the climb with their GoPro cameras to post on their website. We got to know Carlos, an older man who I guessed to be about my age, but that was where the similarities stopped. He was a very experienced climber from Mexico. Having chalked up some incredible climbs in both North and South America, he was here training for his attempt to summit Denali. We met Brandy, a proud alum from University of Alabama, and a second-timer, back to make the summit attempt after coming up short two years earlier due to weather, and Jonathan, a software engineer from Seattle.

The introductions and stories continued for the next several minutes, including my own. The diversity of backgrounds, experience, interests, and motivations were fascinating to me, and it made me even more excited, and somewhat proud, to be included with such an inspiring group of people.

The afternoon proceeded just as Gregg had told us. First, the movie, complete with popcorn and soda. It was a beautifully spectacular video that took us through what was about to unfold. Day Two, our first full day, would be spent in what was called 'snow training.' The actual climb would begin early in the morning of Day Three when we would climb to Camp Muir, base camp for the summit attempt. There we would eat dinner and bunk down for some rest before waking in the wee hours of the morning to make the attempt to gain the summit. It was definitely an eye-opening video, and the butterflies returned briefly, but I felt confident and excited to begin this challenge I had been waiting for, for so many years.

After the video, we all gathered the equipment we would need for the trip from the equipment barn and brought it back to the shelter house. Then, one item at a time, Gregg and Sonya took turns introducing us to each item, demonstrating its purpose, how to use it, and where to place it in our packs for easy retrieval.

Eventually, after another hour or so, after all items were accounted for, Gregg brought the meeting to a close. He clapped his hands once more to get our attention. "Alright, boys and girls, that brings the orientation to a close. But before you go, just remember the most important thing: Our goal is not to reach the summit. Our goal is to attempt to reach the summit and to return everyone safely. We all want to arrive looking good." He paused, nodding his head. "Alright? So, we will meet back here in the morning at 8:00 a.m. for our snow training. OK, now go have a good dinner; it will be your last for the next few days."

We broke camp, grabbed our packs and climbing boots, and went our separate ways for the evening. On the way back to the hotel, I felt a mix of emotions: excitement, fear, confidence, and trepidation. On one hand, I was asking myself "What in the world am I doing here?" On the other hand, I was thinking "This is exactly where you are supposed to be, so embrace the challenge." I was so far out of my comfort zone; my head was spinning but looking forward to what I knew would be one of the greatest learning experiences I would ever have.

Snow Training

Day Two arrived, and on the agenda was an entire day learning the finer points of mountaineering. It was commonly known among the guides as snow training. This was the point in the expedition where the guides took us up the mountain 7,000–7,500 feet, to the edge of the Muir Snowfield, where we would spend the day practicing all necessary climbing techniques, the use of our equipment, climbing in crampons, breaking a fall, ascending and descending while clipped on the rope, and other safety maneuvers that could save our lives. It was severe and challenging stuff, but after repeated practice we managed to become quite proficient, and the guides were finally happy with our performance.

However, what captured my attention were the mountain guides themselves. All along the hike up to the snowfield, each guide would take their time, simply walking and talking with every member of the climbing party. They would ask what we did for a living, where we were from, about family and friends, other interests, and perhaps most importantly, they asked a little more about why we decided to have this adventure. Sometimes, they would point out interesting sights or points of interest along the route or offer tips and insights on how to make the most of the climb. Likewise, I was inspired to learn more about them as well. I was interested to hear their stories about how and why they ended up here, leading groups of adventure seekers to the top of Mt. Rainier. While their stories were certainly unique and fascinating, there seemed to be three common denominators. One was their love for the outdoors, and especially mountains, their love for climbing, and the satisfaction they gained by helping others achieve their goals.

I would only come to realize the significance of those conversations later in our adventure; however, it's worth mentioning that our guides were demonstrating the element of Embrace. They made all team members feel comfortable, appreciated, and valued. Most importantly, it helped everyone relax and feel safe in their presence.

I've watched many exemplary leaders practice the element of Embrace as well. I hope that you have too: those times when your leader has gone out of their way to ensure you feel comfortable, safe and valued. I'd like to share a couple of examples to give you some idea of what this might look like.

These days, we hear a lot about diversity, equity, and inclusion, and rightly so. Most of us aspire to create an organizational culture that embodies these principles. Before DEI, we talked about engagement, and long before that, we discussed employee satisfaction, participation, safety, equality, and loyalty. The core sentiment behind all these efforts is a heartfelt desire to embrace everyone on the team, regardless of any assumptions, and welcome them with open arms.

We should strive to help everyone in the organization feel a sense of belonging, valued for who they are and what they contribute, and, most importantly, feel a sense of psychological safety and personal well-being.

Interestingly, this concept is not new to an Elevated Leader. Reflecting on these modern aspirations beyond the business world, I recall how many of my most admired leaders naturally demonstrated the element of Embrace. Below, I share two examples. First, we'll revisit Jim the GM and see how a simple idea helped build stronger relationships and team spirit. Then, I'll tell you about Paul, the President and COO of a steel coating and treatment company in Ohio, who transformed a caustic organizational culture into one of genuine excellence through the element of Embrace.

Jim's Badges

Sometimes the smallest ideas can make a huge difference in building relationships and making people feel comfortable. This was the case with Jim the GM's badges.

Six months after I started working at Team Columbus, I had just finished our morning production meeting when an announcement came in over the PA system. Connie, our HR Manager, announced that starting at 9:00 am, all employees needed to pick up their new Team Columbus secure ID badges.

Following the instructions, I went to the front office at nine. Connie and her team greeted me warmly, sitting behind tables with a camera tripod, a paper slicer, and a laminating machine. It all looked very official. As I traded in my old badge, Connie asked, "Hi Mark, do you have a preferred name or maybe a nickname you prefer to have on your badge?"

Surprised, I thought for a moment. I had grown familiar with the regular standard badge protocol: Last Name, First Name, Middle Initial. Immediately, I thought of my college nickname. "Sure, how about Moon," I replied.

"Sure, Moon," Connie replied with a smile, and the team went to work. In less than five minutes, I had my new photo taken and my new security ID badge.

Mark "Moon" Mullen
Assembly Team Phoenix

"Well, what do you think?" asked Bernie, Connie's assistant.

"I like it!" I said with a smile. "Aside from the bad photo, I think it looks great." I thanked them and went on my way back to the shop.

This was something new and unique. I looked forward to having my coworkers call me by the same name as my friends, but I had no idea at the time what a huge impact that simple change would have on our workplace culture.

Over the next few weeks, those new badges became quite a thing around the plant. Let's just say there was a lot of badge reading going on. It was fun and comforting to address fellow employees in a way they were most comfortable with, especially those I had only infrequent contact with, or perhaps meeting for the first time. Those badges were a common denominator. They helped us get to know each other on a slightly more personal level. This went a long way in breaking down the old barriers between management and union employees, making it easier to look beyond our differences toward what we had in common as people.

During our next all-hands meeting, Jim, our general manager, mentioned the new badges. "I hope you're all having fun with that—credit Brenda over at Sheet Metal Fab for the idea. I loved it. From this point on, maybe my boss will call me Jim, instead of some of those other names he calls me." That brought a big laugh from everyone, followed by a round of applause.

This simple move, an idea shared by a coworker and implemented by our general manager, was an excellent example of a leader embracing those he led and providing the opportunity for us all to do the same. The result was a milestone at Team Columbus, instrumental in creating an inclusive culture built on trust and respect. The point is, it doesn't take a genius or magic or some rare genetic trait to practice the element of Embrace. All it takes is someone with the right mindset and heartset to demonstrate it for those you lead, whoever that might be.

Paul's Epiphany

Paul, President and Chief Operating Officer of MetaTek, sat in his idling car waiting for the red light to change, but his mind was elsewhere. He had just finished a call with ownership, and it did not go well. For the sixth straight month and the fifteenth time in twenty months, he had the unenviable task of presenting another sub-par performance. With the board meeting just three weeks away, he knew he would have to go in with a plan, or else he was toast.

After receiving a new lease on life, the forty-three-year-old metal processing plant had reopened after a three-year hiatus. In a joint venture between two of the world's largest steel companies, one American, one Japanese, the facility now boasted some of the most advanced and sophisticated metal coating processes and technology in the world. It was located in a small northern Ohio town, full of enthusiastic and eager men and women ready to get back to work. At the opening two years prior, the future had looked bright; however, it often felt as if a dark cloud was hanging overhead. The metal treatment plant under Paul's responsibility had been plagued by production problems, union grievances, poor quality, rework, machine downtime, absenteeism, and missed delivery dates, to name just a few. These were troubling, but perhaps most disturbing to Paul was the toxic workplace culture at the plant.

The age-old conflict between management and the United Steelworkers union had plagued this plant and the industry for years. From the union's perspective, they represented the best interests of their members. "Ah, it's just the same old pig wearing lipstick," was a common refrain that Paul would hear. On the other hand, his managers only saw the union as obstructing their efforts to manage the business, which they believed was in everyone's best interest. One thing was certain: The two sides were mixing like oil and water.

Paul knew the challenge he was stepping into when he accepted the role of MetaTek's first President and COO. He was no stranger to the industry, having grown up around steel and spent his summers working as a laborer, then as a metallurgy intern during college. From his father, he had learned the rough-and-tumble management style that served him well in union dealings. Yet, Paul wasn't sure he wanted to continue that tradition. He believed there had to be a better way. Although he wasn't entirely sure what it would look like, he knew the future was less about good management and more about effective leadership, and he was eager to take on the challenge.

For the first six months or so after opening, things progressed well. The first group of operators and technicians were trained and certified even before the plant went into full production, and they were doing an excellent of passing along their knowledge to the newly hired employees. However, as production and other performance expectations became more challenging, the mood began to sour, with the training program being the first to suffer. The experienced associates were pulled away from training to meet production requirements and satisfy angry customers. Overtime increased, and the start of the third shift was delayed further due to a lack of training for new operators. As other problems mounted, tensions rose, and Paul soon recognized that many of the old attitudes and behaviors had returned. He was afraid that much of the trust that he had worked so hard to gain over the past several months was slowly eroding. There was no need to look for someone or something to blame. Everyone had a hand in allowing the organization's culture to deteriorate to this point, and everyone would have to help improve it.

As he sat waiting for the traffic light to change, Paul realized that he had a leadership void on his hands. In fact, he had several leadership voids, but he knew it started with him. The situation and the circumstances were only going to improve if he made the necessary changes, beginning with himself. He would lean on his experience, not to perpetuate the same old culture, but to change it for the better. At that moment, an idea came to him. Suddenly, he knew exactly what he was going to do as soon as he got back to the plant. Then the light turned green.

The following morning, Paul scheduled a meeting between the plant union officials and his entire management team. The title of the meeting was just two words: Our Culture. He described the purpose of the meeting as "an open discussion regarding our shared leadership responsibility for creating and nurturing the type of culture every employee wants to be a part of."

The following morning, all those invited started to gather and, as usual, took up their battle positions around the conference table. The management team sat on one side of the table with the union representatives on the other, all poised and ready for whatever chaos might ensue. All eyes were on Paul. With animation and some degree of angst, he opened the meeting by leaning on the table with both hands and making his plea. He opened with just five words.

"Folks, I need your help." He paused briefly. "I really do need your help. Let me start by asking you this: Is there anyone here pleased with how things are going around here?"

No one said a word and fourteen pairs of eyes looked away to find some imaginary focal point in the distance.

"Yeah, that's what I thought. Well, I can tell you that I am not happy, and I am sure that many of you and your fellow coworkers are not happy either. Let's face it: this is not a nice place to work right now. We all want the best for all of us. Certainly, that includes how we serve our customers by delivering high-quality steel coatings on time. However, it also includes how we serve each other by working to create the type of place we want to work and build a career."

He paused and raised his hands in the air. "We all know how things have gone in the past regarding our labor–management partnership, and I would like to see if we can work better together for the success of our company."

He gazed around the table, and it was obvious he managed to get everyone's attention. They all started to fidget a bit, with those same grim looks on their faces, betraying their mistrust for each other and for Paul. However, he didn't budge. He waited, silently, gazing around the table. Finally, he managed to get a few nods and shrugs. That was good enough for him to claim progress.

"OK then, I am going to get this all started by asking you all to do me a favor and play a game I have in mind. I will have you pair up with your counterpart across the table. We are going to give you the time between now and 3:00 p.m. tomorrow to meet with your partners to discuss your responses to these three simple questions." He listed them for us:

1) What is one thing you found interesting about your partner you didn't know before?
2) What's one thing you appreciate most about working here?
3) What is one thing that you would like to see change to make this a better place to work?

He gazed around the table again. "We will all meet again tomorrow at 3:00 p.m. to hear about what you learned from each other."

Harley Charley, shop steward for Zone 5, sat near the back, his massive arms crossed strategically across his chest to showcase the work of his tattoo artist. He smirked, "Ahh, come now, you got to be frigging kidding me!" Obviously, he wasn't a fan of the idea. He wasn't one to go for this "warm and fuzzy team building stuff" as he referred to it.

But then Cynthia, Zone 10 manager, spoke up. She was a long-term employee for MetaTek, having joined the company straight out of high school. Three years ago, after twelve years as an hourly employee working in the shop, she eventually took the opportunity to move into management. She was tough as nails. Growing up on a farm as the middle child, two older siblings and two younger, she was a strong, sturdy woman, no stranger to hard work, nor the rough and tough attitudes often encountered in the plant. She knew Charley well and didn't pay much attention to his grumbling. Aside from him being a tough old curmudgeon sometimes, she knew he was a good guy underneath it all and had learned how to deal with him.

"Ah, c'mon, Charley, it ain't gonna hurt you to give this a chance. Stop being so difficult. In fact, if it makes you feel better, I'll even be your partner."

Charley mumbled a little but finally gave in. Then he said jokingly, "What are people going to say if they see me sucking up to my manager? This might ruin my street cred."

Cynthia replied, "Well, I guess that's just the risk you must take to make progress."

Charly just smiled back. "Alright, boss, I'm in."

That seemed to give permission for everyone around the table to relax and let their guard down a bit, but Harley Charley wasn't the only one expressing his skepticism. Clarence, the Facility Maintenance manager, also shared his displeasure with the idea. A rather wiry, thin, Black man, Clarence was never one to keep opinions to himself. He sat forward, arms on the table, tapping his pen on the notebook that lay in front of him. "You know Paul. I have to agree with Charley on this one. This all seems a little too softy-feely to me. How many times have we met to discuss these issues, yet nothing seems to change? It really just comes down to making sure everyone holds up their end to the stick. I mean, c'mon, we all know what the problem is. We have a few bad apples who would rather spend time stirring up trouble and causing conflict by signing grievances instead of putting in an honest day's work. We can't do anything to discipline them without the union running to sign the grievance book. Hell, I spend more time dealing with the grievances than I do managing the facility. I really don't see how this 'dating game' of yours is going to solve these problems." He said this with more than a little cynicism in his voice.

Paul was obviously perturbed by Clarence's comments, but he continued to persist. "I hear you Clarence, and there is a lot of truth to what you are saying. I would guess some of the union shop stewards like Connie and Brad here would agree. I also agree that we have been meeting and discussing these issues for some time now, yet nothing has changed. That is exactly my point. I don't think anything is going to change until *we* all change and try something different."

Clarence shrugged his shoulders, and remained silent, staring at the opposite wall, biting his tongue while he conformed to his boss's wishes.

Everyone else remained silent. The remarks by Charley, Cynthia, Clarence, and Paul seemed to suffice in representing the common sentiment in the room. Finally, although guarded and somewhat reluctant, everyone selected a partner.

Once everyone was paired off, Paul called an end to the meeting. "Before we go, I just want to say that I appreciate all you trying to remain open-minded enough to try this. I think the first thing we need to do is to be honest with ourselves, to recognize our culture for what it is—the good, the bad, and the ugly—, to Embrace our team with all its faults and blemishes, and perhaps most importantly, *embrace* each other for who we are, as people, neighbors, and fellow team members who want to work together to make MetaTek a great place to work."

He paused to gaze around the table again, then continued by pointing to his chest. "This all begins with me. I take full responsibility and intend to do a better job as a leader. Now, I am asking for your help to make it happen."

He raised his finger to emphasize his next point. "I believe the best way to begin working together is to accept each other for who we are and what we bring to the table. Most of us have been together for several years, many of you much longer than I have; however, I wonder just how well we really know each other. So, let's spend a little time getting better acquainted before we dive in to solve this problem that we all are tired of dealing with. Alright?"

He managed to get a few more nodding heads, which he took as an affirmation. "OK then, I'll see you back here tomorrow at the same time. I am looking forward to hearing more about what you discussed. Thanks!"

No one knew what to expect when everyone returned to the follow-up meeting. As the group entered the room, they noticed their nameplates on the table and a single sheet of paper in front of each chair.

"Come on in, everyone, have a seat," Paul was saying as he shook everyone's hand. That was different. Most of them were surprised that he would even offer a handshake. Charley gave him a second look, probably wondering whether he had any additives for his usual *venti* Starbucks coffee. Nonetheless, he had them take a seat, instructing them to turn over the paper in front of them only when asked.

Paul took a position at the front of the room, flanked by three flip charts. At the top of each chart were each of the three questions he had set out before. On flip chart one: One thing you found interesting about your partner that you didn't know before. On flip chart two: One thing that you appreciate most about working here. On flip chart three: One thing you would like to make this a better place to work.

"OK, the last time we were together for this meeting, you all had a special, good-faith assignment. I hope you all had time to discuss those questions with your partner. Now, I would like to hear what each pair has come up with."

The first question sparked a fun and lively conversation, with each pair taking turns sharing something new they learned about their partners. For instance, they discovered that Connie, the union shop steward, was a professional pianist. Karl was a chainsaw sculptor and had won several awards for his craftsmanship. Jeremy had spent three years in Manila as a missionary and schoolteacher, while Carol, a machine operator in Zone 3, was a sports car race driver who owned two vintage Porshe 911s. Terry's hobby was taking vacations to Hollywood to try making casting calls for movie and TV extras. He was proud to mention that had appeared "oh-so briefly" in one movie and two sitcoms.

The conversations were engaging and quite entertaining, with everyone fully engaged eager to share. Obviously, the first question had served its purpose. The mood in the room had changed dramatically since the day before with everyone having a little fun as they learned something new and personal about each other. As a result, everyone was more relaxed and open to sharing. Paul was hoping that it would lead to better collaboration in the future.

Eventually, in the interest of time, he had to intervene, "Alright, this is a great start. Now, let's move on to the other two questions, beginning with Question Two." He walked over to the second flip chart and pulled the cap off the marker. "OK, now what is the one thing you appreciate most about working at MetaTek?" he asked the group. "Let's go around the table and hear what you all came up with." Paul turned to Carol, who was sitting directly to his left. "Carol, let's start with you."

As the conversation continued, each pair of partners shared their answers, and Paul diligently recorded their remarks on the flip chart, noting a short list of three recurring themes.

- It's the best job in town. Better than working at McDonalds
- Enjoy the work. – It really is kind of cool what we do here. It's a good job.
- A paycheck and benefits. Health care, paid time off.

Once Paul had finished with his note taking, he then turned to the third flip chart. "Alrighty then, now, how about the last and most important question. What is the one thing you would like to change to make this a better place to work?

This time, instead of an orderly process of going around the table, a lively discussion broke out immediately. Paul thought it healthy, so he just let the conversation go, taking notes as he went along. There was plenty of midwestern, blue-color banter and debate, but it was all good-natured, organically stimulating, productive, and collaborative, producing what appeared to be a manageable laundry list of items everyone would like to change for the better. Surprising to some, not so much to others, there was much in common.

- No more finger-pointing and blaming others for problems; being accountable.
- Responsibility and accountability for getting the job done.
- 100% On-time delivery. Happy customers versus angry customers – or no customers at all.
- Focus on getting more people trained in the different processes. Training, training, training.
- Better relationships, especially between management and the union. More open communication and transparency. No more 'us' and 'them.'
- Better teamwork and problem solving between departments.
- No more mandatory overtime.

After the conversation ended, Paul finished catching up with the notes. He turned and faced the group, then back to the flip charts. "Well, that is quite a list, but it sure sounds great.

"I don't know about you, but I think we learned a lot in the past twenty minutes. One, we learned more about each other as people, not just coworkers: your family, your experiences, your hobbies and pastimes, and much more. Two, I've learned a lot about what we are grateful for, working here at MetaTek. And three, what it is going to take to make this a better place to work."

He paced in front of the room for a few moments, staring down at the floor. Then he looked up and pointed to the third flip chart. "Now, the last question I have for you is this: What will each of you do to make this a reality?"

The group sat silently as they contemplated that last question. By the look of bewilderment on each face, Paul was sure that no one had a good answer, as he anticipated.

He paused for a few seconds, continuing to look around the room. Then, finally, he started up again. "OK, so maybe you don't have an answer yet. That's OK, we can talk about that later."

Paul returned to the first flip chart and turned to a blank page. He proceeded to draw a rather feeble depiction of a mountain. "The point of me asking each of you that question is because if we are going to turn this thing around at MetaTek, we have a huge mountain to climb. As for me, I intend to do just that, but no one makes it to the summit alone. It takes a team. It takes time and persistence. It takes determination and lots of hard work, but most of all it takes leadership. A team of leaders.

"That is where you come in. I see this group gathered right here as our climbing team, a team of leaders, and what you have here in front of you can all be boiled down to one simple thing: Leadership. What we have here at MetaTek is a leadership void—several leadership voids in fact. Do you know what a leadership void is? That means the need for leadership is going unmet.

"So, to begin with, that void begins with me, and I intend to fill it, however, I cannot fill this void alone. I am going to need your help. Every one of you. We are the plant leadership team, and the change we want will have to begin with us. Suppose we work together as a team of leaders to achieve some all these things." He turned to the flip chart and drew a staggered line from the bottom of his mountain to the summit. "If we do so, I have no doubt that we will reach the summit, which means a world-class facility with a culture everyone wants to be a part of."

He paused briefly and clasped his hands. "Alright, you can turn over the document in front of you and give it a read."

Turning over the document, they saw written there a personal declaration of sorts.

I, _____, AM FULLY COMMITTED TO BEING A LEADER AT METATEK, AND I WILL DO WHAT IT TAKES TO HELP MY COLLEAGUES SUCCEED IN MAKING METATEK AN INDUSTRY LEADER AND A GOOD PLACE TO WORK FOR ALL ASSOCIATES.

SIGNATURE: _____

Once again, he got a round of blank stares and even a few more smirks.

Harley Charley had to speak up again. "Ah, c'mon Paul, now what is this all about? What if we refuse to sign?"

Paul shrugged, "That's OK, that's your prerogative; at least I know that we need not count on you for leadership." He said this only half-jokingly. He still had that edge when bantering with the contrarians. "Listen, Charley, let me explain. What we have here is a terrible situation for everyone involved. We are battling for the existence of our plant and all our livelihoods. I don't know how else to put it. That is how bad things are at this point. The bottom line is not just our dismal performance month over month, but that we all acknowledge this is not a very nice place to work. Why is that?"

Charley just shrugged, "It's a combination of many things, I guess."

"I agree," Paul replied, "it is a host of things we see occur regularly, but I have concluded it all boils down to one thing: Leadership. That's it! You could say that I haven't provided enough leadership, and you would be correct. I take full responsibility for that. However, no single person, no individual leader, can fill every leadership void in this organization. It is going to take a team, a team of leaders, to do that, and that is where you come in. So again, I am asking for your help to be a leader, to do your part, and to change things for the better." He pointed to the managers and union officers sitting around the table. "Can I count on you?"

Slowly, reluctantly, they all nodded their heads.

"OK, great!"

Once they had all signed the pledge, Paul picked it up again. "Now, obviously, this is not a legally binding contract. It is simply a pledge that we are making to embrace the situation at hand for what it is and acknowledge each other as leaders and team members. Like it or not, this is reality, and the sooner we embrace it, the sooner we can begin our climb to the top of this mountain standing before us."

This story was shared with me by a few of those who were involved some twenty months after it occurred. Since that time, MetaTek had experienced an incredible turnaround. Plant performance improved significantly regarding productivity, efficiency, and first-time quality, all critical customer-focused metrics. Just as importantly, smiles had returned to the faces of those who worked there, evidenced by their winning the award for being one of Ohio's best places to work as well as the Ohio Partnership for Excellence's Governors Award and the national Malcolm Baldrige Award for Excellence. Paul had come to realize that he had no choice but to leave behind those ghosts of management past and demonstrate the element of Embrace among his entire organization.

In the same way, the professional mountain guide rarely has the opportunity to select members of the climbing team. If what I experienced is typical, climbing parties are often the model of diversity, with adventurers coming from all walks of life.

Elevated Leaders look forward and look up. They must embrace the situation, their team, and every climber before moving forward with the expedition. That is why they take as much time as they have to get to know every team member—their background, their experience, their capability, and perhaps most importantly, their personality—and what is driving them to do what they are doing. Like a mountain guide preparing his climbing party to reach the summit of their performance, Paul was doing the same thing, practicing the element of Embrace.

Forrest Gump once said, "Life is like a box of chocolates. You never know what you're going to get." One could say the same about our teams and those we work with. So, like Forrest Gump, let's embrace it.

CHAPTER SEVEN

Empower

Empower those you lead by providing the knowledge, information, tools, and personal development resources needed to be successful.

Empowering employees can greatly enhance their willingness to exceed expectations in their roles, leading to increased job satisfaction and productivity. Conversely, when employees lack empowerment, they may become disengaged, which can be costly for organizations due to lost productivity and higher recruitment expenses.

Empowering others involves recognizing that success is not achieved in isolation; it requires collective effort supported by leadership. Elevated leaders enable individuals to reach their full potential by providing access to essential knowledge, information, and developmental resources.

Empowerment goes beyond simply delegating tasks or assigning responsibilities; it's about instilling confidence and autonomy in team members. It involves fostering a culture where individuals feel empowered to take initiative, confidently make decisions, and contribute meaningfully to the organization's goals.

In today's rapidly evolving world, continuous learning and development are more critical than ever. Elevated Leaders prioritize personal development resources for their teams, whether through training programs, mentorship opportunities, or access to educational materials. They ensure that their team members have the tools and knowledge they need to succeed.

Ultimately, empowerment is about creating an environment where individuals feel respected, supported, and equipped to thrive. By empowering those they lead, Elevated Leaders lay the foundation for a culture of innovation, collaboration, and continuous improvement, where every team member is motivated to do their best work.

Rainier, Day Two: Ascension

Now, it was getting real. Day Two of my Rainier summit climb meant the beginning of the ascent, starting up the mountain at Paradise Inn and ending at Camp Muir, the summit base camp at 10,188 feet above sea level. I can vividly recall the thoughts and emotions going through my mind on the drive to our gathering place, Rainier Mountain Guide's headquarters where we were to catch the bus to Paradise Inn. Behind the wheel of the rental car, I had this strong sense of empowerment. Finally, I was ready to experience what it is like to climb that magnificent, glaciated mountain.

Due to the rigorous preparation and comprehensive training we received from our mountain guides, I felt a strange mix of emotions—I was both enabled and capable, yet overwhelmed by a deep-seated fear. While I was undeniably motivated, I couldn't shake the gnawing anxiety that gripped me. The prospect of the unknown loomed large, and for the first time in my life, I genuinely questioned whether I might return to see my wife and family. It wasn't just a fleeting thought; it was a visceral fear that weighed heavily on my mind. It added a sobering reality to the adventure ahead. I did my best to push these thoughts to the back of my mind, recognizing that fear was a natural part of any challenge.

As I arrived at the main base camp to join the team, any lingering doubts were eclipsed by the sense of camaraderie and purpose that permeated the atmosphere. My guides, seasoned and confident, gave me a unanimous vote of confidence. Their trust in my abilities was both humbling and empowering. I was a full-fledged member of the climbing team. This newfound sense of belonging carried with it a profound responsibility. The team would depend on me, just as I would depend on them, to contribute to the success of our expedition. The weight of this responsibility was daunting, yet it fueled my determination to rise to the challenge, knowing that we were all in this together, bound by a shared goal and an unwavering commitment to each other's safety and success.

Empowering others can be risky business, but Elevated Leaders understand it is a risk that they must take if they are going to be successful.

Elevated Leaders are humble enough to grasp the obvious fact that no one leader can fill all the leadership voids that occur on a regular basis. Those who think they can go it alone rarely reach the summit. Elevated Leaders recognize and embrace that risk by showing confidence in those they lead, empowering them, and trusting them to do the right thing. They will use their intellect, knowledge, experience, and intuition to ask the right questions and find the correct answers. Some may stumble. Some might fall short, yet lessons are always learned.

The All-Hands Meeting

I stood frozen on the stage, flanked by the other five team members on both sides. We had just completed our presentation for the monthly review, addressing Jim, our general manager, along with several hundred other associates during the company's "all hands" meeting. This meeting required a select number of teams to report on their key performance indicators, including new orders, completed orders, work in progress, quality, on-time delivery, scrap, and rework, among others. Overall, our team had much to be proud of, having met or exceeded expectations for the seventh consecutive month.

However, one particularly challenging job had become a significant issue. A highly technical step in the assembly process was causing repeated delays every time we encountered it. This problem had persisted since the first shipset arrived at the plant. We had notified the engineers, and a change notice was in progress. But that was two months ago, and since then, our team had more or less adapted to dealing with the issue whenever the job came up.

After I shared the details about this problematic job, Jim raised his hand for a question. A wave of anxiety hit me; there was no such thing as a simple question from Jim. He was always at least three steps ahead of everyone else in the room.

"Hi, Jim," I said, pointing to him to ask his question.

"So, what will you and your team do about this problem?" he asked.

Standing on the stage, I was put on the spot to provide an answer, so I gave it my best shot. "Well, we had Dave and Liz stop by from Engineering to look at the assembly and the process steps. Gabe and Nico from Tooling were brought in to see if there were some adjustments that we needed to make to the fixture. The team suggested looking at the sequence of steps earlier in the process or re-engineering that part of the tool, but that would mean talking to the technicians back in St Louis."

I was hoping that was the correct answer, but it wasn't.

Jim nodded his head and looked down at the table. "And how has that worked out for you?" he asked as he reviewed some of the documentation regarding the problem.

I stammered out my answer, trying not to point fingers in front of the entire group. "Well, we still have the problem."

Then he said, "OK, thank you, Team 7. You're doing a nice job overall, but we need to get you some help on this one."

Then he stood up and removed his reading glasses. He walked to the center of the room, where he started to address the crowd situated around the room, team by team. His finger went up to emphasize what he was about to say. You could see that he was doing his best to hold back the frustration that was etched on his face.

He took a deep breath and began, "OK, folks, ladies, gentlemen, teammates. This is a prime example of what we are trying to change here at Team Columbus. You know we spend a lot of time talking about empowerment. But do we understand what that means and how to do it? There is no need to answer. The answer is no. I don't think so."

He said, "When encountering a problem, we must establish ownership. Who is going to claim this as their problem? Is it the assembly team? Is it management? Is it Engineering? Is it Tooling?" He paused and looked around the room. "Those are not rhetorical questions! Tell me, anyone! Who should have ownership of this problem?"

Some shouted out, "Management!"

Some shouted out, "Engineering!"

Gabe shouted out, "It's Tooling. We always get the blame."

"Nah, it's St. Louis," Jennifer said sarcastically. "We have been trying to get them involved, but they say it's 'not their problem,'" she said, signaling air quotes with her fingers.

"Wrong!" Jim exclaimed, his finger pointing back toward the stage. "This team owns this problem, whether it realizes it or not. Why? This team is feeling the pain from all the workarounds, change notices, and delays. Sure, management needs to be there to support and provide the resources they need to overcome this challenge. The engineers are there to assist, provide expertise, and enable the team to make the changes that they believe are needed. Tooling, you might be able to help."

He returned to his seat behind the cafeteria table, but before taking a seat, he gave us our instructions. "Team 7, I want you to continue pursuing the possible causes you spoke of. Even better, perhaps some potential solutions. I'll leave it to you to determine what support you might need from George, your manager, Engineering, whomever. We will be sure to get it for you. Also, in the meantime, I'll arrange to set up a direct communication line between your team and the assembly team leader back in St Louis. Feel free to reach out to them as needed."

I stood before my team, listening to our instructions and nodding, but I couldn't help feeling bewildered. Looking at my teammates, they shared my confusion. This was entirely new to us. We were not used to being empowered to act and make decisions regarding the issues we encountered daily on the assembly floor. We were accustomed to focusing solely on our designated tasks, leaving the problems to be dealt with by someone else. But now, we had been given the responsibility, resources, and accountability to make a difference.

Over the next few weeks, a problem-solving team was formed, with fully dedicated resources from Tooling and Engineering, to address the issues troubling us. We even had an engineer and two mechanics fly in from St. Louis to work with the team to resolve the problem. Finally, the team arrived at a permanent solution to the problem, a combination of actions everyone involved took. It was quite a remarkable experience to see things come together like they did, all because Jim had empowered the team to do so.

Jim had a clear vision of how things would work at Team Columbus and the type of culture he wanted to cultivate: one in which people are empowered to step up as leaders, lean in, and take ownership of opportunities to reach higher levels of success. John applied the element of empowerment, much like the mountain guides of Mt. Rainier.

Going with the Flow

When I first met Mariah, I never would have guessed that she was the lead engineer at Axiom. She was a thin young woman of Native American descent, standing about five feet tall, with long black hair in a ponytail that reached down to the small of her back, pinned in place with a Cincinnati Reds baseball cap. Her safety glasses looked two sizes too big for her face.

She met me in the lobby, stretching out her hand, with a big smile. "You must be Mark. I'm Mariah. I am so glad you are here. We have much to show you."

I was visiting Axiom as part of a regular six-month organizational assessment to review progress on the implementation of our company's business excellence system, or BES. The process typically involves reviewing operational performance, providing updates on performance improvement initiatives, and creating action plans for the next six months.

It was rare to receive such a welcome reception at Axiom. Up until his retirement in July of the same year, Barry, the founder, president, and CEO of this very successful business unit, often looked upon these visits as another example of Corporate interfering with his operation. Now, when he wasn't spending his time playing golf, fishing, and smoking fine cigars, he was there in his office "overseeing the transition," to use his term.

He was a nice enough guy, but a formidable man to deal with and would offer his hospitality only long enough for me to gather the information I needed to meet all of the system requirements, but never more. I learned with Barry to be happy with what he did provide.

But Mariah was different, vastly different. She had been hand-picked by Barry to be his successor. He claimed that she not only had technical and business skills, but that she had something he did not. He called it "a way with people," and within the first hour of that visit, I could see what he was talking about. Mariah had a warm but energetic personality that people could relate to and rally around. She had definitely won the trust of Barry as well as everyone else in the business.

As was typical during one of these visits, the implementation team would begin by sharing the results of their most recent value stream analysis. In Axiom's case, this analysis had been started during my previous visit three months prior and was completed not long after. The initial results of the study were not surprising to anyone on the team.

Lead times on work orders of $100K or more were averaging just over 47 days. This was an increase of 123% over the previous two years, the outcome of positive risk you could say. Business had never been better. However, the shop was taking on more work than it could handle, resulting in a backlog of projects that stretched out for nine months. Unfortunately, this led to an increase in the cost of doing business. People were overworked, with most employees working six or seven days a week. However, this increase in hours didn't result in a significant rise in overall productivity. The lack of productivity made increasing the shop's capacity and shortening lead times difficult. The technicians were experiencing countless interruptions due to incomplete information required to complete the process.

Meanwhile, engineers were frustrated with the growing number of change requests due to errors and omissions on the work orders. As a result, on-time delivery of completed orders was now below 90%. This situation was unacceptable at Axiom, and customers were unhappy with the service they were receiving.

The problem was traced to the very beginning of the process where the project sales team would gather customer requirements on each order and enter them into the Enterprise Resource Planning, or ERP, system as an active work order. Once entered, the orders were picked up by the production manager who then distributed the work according to those requirements, which usually included a mix of both manufacturing and critical testing.

Over the past year or so, the team had almost tripled, and sixteen team members had been added. The inexperience was beginning to show itself. This was challenging; customer requirements were typically precise, requiring attention to detail and the salespeople had to know enough to ask the right questions. If you did not know the answer, you would never guess. You had to search until you found the answer.

Even though it was a team of twenty-one people, most if not all of these answers came from the original "Fab Four" as they liked to call themselves. James, Nancy, Dee, and Bonnie were the first four employees that Barry hired when he started the business. The value that their knowledge and experience provided for the business was beyond measure.

However, with the steady increase in orders, the original Fab Four, once the enabler of the process, had now become the bottleneck. They simply could not keep up with the volume of work coming in. To compound the problem, the company operated with an old version of the ERP system that Barry himself had purchased and configured years ago. This system was quite unique and fit the needs of the business in years past but was now in need of an update or a replacement. Despite its advanced features, its flaws and shortcomings became apparent over the past couple years as the business grew. The work order process was affected, and the weaknesses in the system became more noticeable. These were the issues facing the business, and I was about to hear directly from the entire team what it had done and was doing to improve those results.

I followed Mariah back through the hallways, a left and then a right, to get to the conference room.

"Come on in and have a seat," Mariah said, pointing to one of the eight conference room chairs. I took the third one from the front on the right.

"We are so glad you are here. The team can't wait to show you what we've been up to since your last visit." Raising her finger, she added, "Let me round up the team, and we'll get started. There should be some coffee and morning munchies coming in soon."

I waved and smiled, "Alright, I could use some coffee."

It wasn't five minutes before she returned, joined by Karen, director of project sales; Yao from engineering; Sammy, shop floor coordinator; and Bonnie, one of the original Fab Four: these folks made up the OpEx implementation team for Axiom. After a brief five minutes of small talk and shop talk, Mariah was ready to begin the presentation.

"Let me begin by summarizing the results of our previous OpEx review," Mariah stated as she advanced the slide, displaying critical metrics from the report. "There were no surprises. Over the past few months, it has become increasingly clear that our business is growing and requires some changes. In short, if we continue to operate as we have been, we risk missing out on this growth opportunity and jeopardizing the long-term sustainability of our business."

Karen then got up from her chair. Mariah advanced to the next slide, which showed a visual of the value stream, with one area circled and highlighted, then handed Karen the clicker.

Karen picked up the thread. "We identified several points early in the value stream where project orders are taken and entered into the ERP system for release to the test floor. The issues that we have identified are included here in our report. Extensive delays are caused by errors, omissions, and bad data, accounting for up to 65% of our overall lead time before the order is released to the floor. This is where we have focused our efforts on making the necessary changes that will help us process our orders in such a way as to reduce the time on every order."

Karen advanced the slide and handed the clicker to Yao, the process engineer. Yao was a slim, energetic young man who emigrated from Taiwan to finish grad school. He had a particular talent for describing the actual changes to the process workflow, including changes to the physical office space.

Yao explained that after studying the process and all available data, they had concluded that the root cause of the problems was a lack of knowledge and effective decision-making among the project sales and order entry team. This was no surprise to anyone in the room. He then pointed to the diagrams on the screen and explained that Requests for Proposals (RFPs) were indiscriminately entered into the backlog, regardless of size and complexity. Each team member would select the next RFP in queue and enter data into the system. While this ensured that orders were taken up and started as soon as possible, it also contributed to the busy and chaotic environment in the office.

Yao paused for a moment, gazed at the screen as if to gather his thoughts. Then he went on. "The only problem is that all project orders are treated differently. Some are small and simple, with few familiar requirements. Some projects are bigger and more complex, requiring a higher level of knowledge and a more detailed user experience in the ERP. Then there are some projects, which we are getting more of, that are very big, with multiple and varied requirements. These orders require the highest degree of knowledge of the products and lengthy, detailed entries into ERP. Until now, whoever took ownership of that RFP was responsible for its completion and release to the floor. If they had a question or needed further information or assistance, one of the Fab Four would typically break away from what they were working on to assist their teammate." Yao paused, with arms outstretched. "That's good, right?"

Several of us nodded our heads, but then Yao smiled and said, "No, that is not good! Not anymore. With the increase in our workload and the sheer number of projects coming through, this is just not sustainable, and as a result, we have a lot of waste in our process."

Yao pointed to the diagram showing how orders flowed from one step to the other and how they often got passed between team members in a quest to get all the necessary information, which caused many handoffs, delays, or even stoppages in the flow of work.

Yao paused, then returned to those of us gathered around the room. "Now, this is where Bonnie comes in." He handed the clicker to Bonnie, who had been sitting quietly at the front of the table with a few papers and a copy of our review report. Bonnie stood up and turned to the audience somewhat reluctantly. This was not something that she was accustomed to, providing a presentation in front of several managers and a visitor from Corporate.

She started out slowly with a little southern drawl, "Hello, everyone. It's good to be with y'all this morning. I want to point out to you this morning some of the amazing changes we have made both in the office and in the shop that have really made a difference in how we have handled orders. Before I start, however, on behalf of the team, I want to thank all of you here this mornin', especially Mariah here." She flashed her a quick smile. "We were unsure what to expect when Mariah was first brought in as our new VP of operations. Heck, this is the first time we have had a director of operations!" She shrugged and smiled again at Mariah. "But things really started to change not long after she arrived. I recall the day that she came to our morning production meeting carrying a bag full of bagels and cream cheese, only to find out that most of the team was more of the "doughnut type." She will never live that down, even though the team would eventually destroy that bag of bagels. More important than the bagels was the reason she came to the meeting—to ask for our help."

Bonnie clicked the slide, again displaying a long list of problems associated with the flow of orders through the system. She continued, "Believe me, none of these problems were new to us. Many of them date as far back as when I first started at Axiom…. We won't mention how long ago that was." Another grin.

"As Yao mentioned, it has only recently become a big problem due to the sheer number of projects coming through the door and the inexperience of our project sales team. Another big part of it is Barry's reluctance to make any changes to what had always worked before." Again, she shrugged. "Well, we all know Barry, right? We all love the guy. It is his business, but the smartest thing he ever did was hire Mariah. He realized that some new, fresh perspectives and expertise might be just what the doctor ordered, giving him more time for golf and fine cigars.

"Anyway, Mariah certainly brought a new approach. I think what surprised all of us that morning while chomping on bagels was that Mariah had come to us asking for help in solving these problems. That was like a breath of fresh air for many of us because we certainly believed we had some good ideas to bring to the table. She basically said, 'Here's the problem. We are depending on this team to solve it.'" Once more, Bonnie glanced at Mariah again. "Thank you, Mariah, for taking that risk, but I assured you that the team would come through, even if we would end up driving Yao crazy in the process." We all laughed at the look on Yao's face. He was nodding his head vigorously.

Bonnie, with the clicker in hand, advanced to the next slide, which showed another version of the office diagram. This one was much different from the first, showing three distinct areas with a block of eight desks facing one another, forming a triangle, and a circular meeting table set in the center of the triangle. A series of arrows represented how the orders flowed through the office in three different streams.

"What you see here is the new office configuration that we have devised. Based on current knowledge and capabilities, we have broken the group into three different teams. Team One will service our small-to medium-sized RFPs and subsequent orders. Team Two will service our medium-to-larger projects. Team Three is comprised of—guess who?—yep, the Fab Four." Bonnie pumped her fist. "We will be handling only the largest, most complex projects."

She described the changes in more detail but saved the best for last. Bonnie and Mariah took me on a tour to showcase the extraordinary changes that the team made to the office itself. As we "walked the process" through the office, there were clear visuals indicating where each project was in the process and how it was tracking against the plan. Most interesting was the triage table in the center. Whenever a project fell behind or was even at risk of doing so, the team would call a huddle and invite others as needed to jump in to get the project back on track. It was truly an ingenious concept, but best of all, it was working exceptionally well. Barry's beloved ERP system was still intact; it was just being used more efficiently.

All the changes to the process and the way the team was working were having incredibly positive results. Productivity had improved substantially. First-time quality was 93%, while the all-important, on-time delivery was 100% for the third straight month. All this is in light of the project backlog still running at historically high levels.

Most important, however, was what I heard from team members, beginning with Bonnie.

"It really has been quite amazing what has happened around here since Mariah came on board. That day, she came to the team with her big old box of bagels. Everything started to change around here, and it all started with her simply asking us for help and empowering us to do what was needed to get things in order. She made it very clear to us that morning that we had big problems, much too big for her or the management team to solve. She was going to need our help."

"That was quite a different tune than the one played for years at Axiom," Bonnie said. It had always been Barry's and the management team's job to run the business and solve any problems that arose. "Our job was to keep turning out job orders and satisfying the customers. Management rarely asked for our input, ideas, or suggestions, and everyone seemed comfortable with how things were. This approach had proven successful for nearly ten years, but it wasn't until the past six months to a year, with the phenomenal growth we've had, that it became apparent that our problems were much deeper than Barry or the management team had previously imagined.

"Mariah was a breath of fresh air. When she came to our team meeting asking for help, we were all surprised and a bit skeptical. However, after she laid out all the problems and issues, it was clear that she and our management team were really struggling to right the ship. She honestly believed that with our help, we could get to the root cause of the problem and come up with solutions."

Bonnie explained how, over the following weeks, Mariah led the team through several Kaizen events focused on creating a continuous, uninterrupted flow of orders through the process, eliminating non-value-added work, and improving first-time quality. "Our team was given a budget of $85,000 and we were empowered to make any changes that we felt were necessary to create better flow, from receiving the RFPs to releasing orders to the shop floor. We were also empowered to reorganize the office to facilitate the process changes and reassign team members to support these structural changes."

The Axiom team responded positively to this new approach to managing the operation. They were given ownership of the processes and finally had a voice in managing the business. Mariah trusted the team to develop an effective and sustainable solution, setting aside her ego and the status quo. The operational results showed a significant improvement, which was truly amazing. However, what mattered most was that Mariah and the entire Axiom team demonstrated the element of empowerment and the positive difference it can make in how we feel about our work and the people we work with.

CHAPTER EIGHT

Engage

Take the first step to build relationships with others.
Touch the heart before asking for a hand.

Leaders should engage with those they lead by providing their time and attention and by actively participating and collaborating in the job at hand. Engagement is about doing something meaningful together.

Employee engagement has become a vital indicator of organizational health, yet only a small percentage of employees are truly engaged at work. Despite efforts over the past decade, engagement levels have remained stagnant, with a significant portion of the workforce feeling disengaged. This disengagement has substantial financial implications, leading to a significant loss in productivity and profitability for businesses.

Engagement encompasses more than just employee participation; it reflects their commitment, loyalty, and overall well-being. It's about how employees feel about their workplace, the tasks they perform, and their relationships with colleagues. More than a mere metric, engagement represents the collective effort to achieve something meaningful.

Leadership plays the most critical role in influencing employee engagement. Within the framework of Elevated Leadership, engagement is not just about gathering employee feedback; it's about actively participating with those you lead and showing a genuine commitment to shared goals. Elevated Leaders understand that true engagement is essential for building trust, fostering collaboration, and driving meaningful action. They know that creating a deeply engaged workforce is not just about meeting targets, but about cultivating an environment where every team member feels valued, motivated, and connected to a larger purpose.

By investing time and energy into their teams, Elevated Leaders inspire others to do the same, fostering a sense of shared purpose and ownership. In today's fast-paced world, effective engagement is more critical than ever. Elevated Leaders prioritize meaningful connections, ensuring every team member feels heard, valued, and appreciated. They understand their team's aspirations, nurturing a culture of empathy, trust, and mutual respect. Ultimately, engagement creates an environment where everyone is inspired and empowered to contribute their best, laying the foundation for collaboration, innovation, and success.

Camp Muir

After a long day of traversing the Muir Snowfield, we finally reached Camp Muir. This bustling base camp serves as the starting point for most climbers attempting to summit Mt. Rainier. The camp was alive with activity, as climbers took time to eat and rest in preparation for the challenging ascent ahead. As evening twilight settled in, we watched the sun dip below the western horizon, casting a golden glow over the valley below.

The peaceful scene lasted about an hour before the clanking of a cowbell broke the silence. It was 6:00 p.m., signaling the time for our final huddle with the climbing team and our guides. This meeting was crucial as we prepared ourselves, both mentally and physically, for the final leg of the journey—the summit attempt.

Once everyone was gathered inside the bunkhouse's spartan confines, our lead guide, Gregg, spoke up to gain our attention. "OK, so how's everyone doing?"

We all responded with varying degrees of enthusiasm—a sign of how tired many of us were.

Gregg shouted, saying it again. "How's everyone doing?"

We gave him a much more convincing response as he finally grabbed our attention. "Looking good, Gregg!"

"OK, my friends. I hope you're all finding the accommodations in accord with expectations. Welcome to the pampered life of a mountaineer," he said, with a big grin on his face.

His attempt at humor fell a little short. No one appeared to be in the mood for it. It was time to get serious.

He quickly became more solemn. "Before we let you go for the night, we wanted to inform you of a few important highlights of what you can expect during our summit attempt."

Pulling himself up with the ease of a chimpanzee, he took a seat perched high above everyone else, then continued. "Shortly after eleven o'clock tonight, we will start checking the weather conditions out on the mountain and communicating with our base station back in Ashford to check for any nasty weather. Before deciding what time to set off for the summit attempt, we will look for a window of fair weather to ensure a safe trip to the top and back to base camp. As soon as our guides agree that conditions are conducive for a safe trip, which could be anytime between 11:00 p.m. and 3:00 am, we will knock on the door with your morning wake-up call. When that happens, you must wake up and begin preparations immediately for the final climb. Time is of the essence.

"Thirty minutes after the wake-up call, we will start the ascent. You'll need to gear up and grab a quick bite to eat. By 'gear up,' I mean crampons, heavy parkas, helmets, headlamps, etcetera. We will empty our packs of all unneeded weight. Any questions about that?" He paused for a few seconds, and after receiving none, he reached out and grabbed the climbing rope that KM had been using to impress us with his knot-tying prowess.

Gregg held out the rope, made a loop, and then clicked it into the clip on his safety belt to make his next point. "From this point on, we will be climbing 'on the rope.' By that, I mean we will be 'hooked in,' tethered to one another in groups of five to seven climbers, with a lead guide in front and a trailing guide behind. We will be engaged in this climb together, working together, and our success will depend on helping each other out when needed and asking for help when needed." Then, with his dry, witty humor, he remarked, "And you thought mountain climbing was an individual sport. Well, I am sorry to disappoint you. Welcome to the team!"

Next, Gregg outlined the plan. "We will set off across Emmons Glacier, where you can expect to encounter the first of a few crevasses. Sometimes, we cross via a natural ice bridge or cross the ladders the trail monitors have laid for us. As we make our way to the summit, we will encounter a challenging section of our climb, lovingly referred to as Disappointment Cleaver. It's challenging enough with plenty of snow cover. Still, it's been made even more challenging this season due to the lack of snowfall accumulation. There will be a lot of exposed, sharp, and uneven surfaces along the trail. As you climb, keep your eyes on the climber in front, following your buddy's steps as closely as possible. This helps the team climb safely and efficiently. We will also be encountering several dangerous crevasses along the way. Fortunately, your friendly trail hands have gone ahead and will lay ladders where needed to bridge these crevasses. If something happens, a slip, a fall, don't panic. Hold your ground as quickly as you can. The team is there whenever any one of us might fall. That way, we all arrive looking good." He smiled, then took a seat. "Any questions about what I just covered?"

He was met with silence, and it was obvious that everyone in the bunkhouse knew that it was about to get real, real soon.

"All right, good. Just a couple more things. First, is there anything that any of you would like to share with the rest of the team before we begin the climb? What I mean, is there anything we all need to be aware of regarding your current condition? Now is the time to talk about it."

The bunkhouse went silent for a few seconds, and a thought entered my mind. I was thinking about the slight weakness in my left ankle that had developed over the past few years because of an injury. I felt compelled to share, but before I could speak up, Brandy beat me to it. She raised her hand, then said, "Yeah, Gregg, I have been dealing with a slight hamstring pull, and I've decided to stay put here at Camp Muir."

Gregg nodded, "I understand," he said. "Probably a good decision. Thanks." Then he waited for any other comments.

Next, Carlos spoke up. "Gregg, I'll be staying behind as well. I'm having some real issues with my stamina right now. I'm not sure what it is, but I think I'll just sit this one out as well."

Gregg nodded. Alright, well I am sorry to hear that, but I thank you for your honesty and letting us know."

Gregg paused again, "Anyone else, questions, comments?"

That's when I raised my hand to speak. Gregg nodded, then I proceeded to share, "I just want to let you know that I do have a slight weakness in my left ankle due to an old back injury. I don't think it will be a problem, but I just thought you should know."

"OK, well, thanks for letting us know," he replied. "If you think you're good to go, that's all we need to hear. But we will definitely keep an eye on it."

After that, there were no more comments. Following a brief silence, Gregg went on. "One more thing. We will be making just one stop on the way up. We will be checking in with everyone to see how you are doing. If, for any reason, you find yourself struggling, you must inform your guides. We realize that everyone here is intent on reaching the summit. Still, more importantly, we should be intent on returning safely to those who are waiting for us back home."

He paused, gazing around the room. "Understood?"

Everyone nodded their head.

"OK, great. Now it's time to try and get some sleep. I hope you brought your earplugs, because the bunkhouse can get really noisy at night with all of the snoring."

That brought a big chuckle from the team and helped to lighten the mood just a bit before we all crawled off into our sleeping bags to try and get a little sleep before engaging in the summit attempt.

Our mountain guides exemplified the core element of engagement through their unwavering commitment to our climbing team's success. From Gregg's spirited briefings to their meticulous attention to detail, they cultivated a strong sense of unity and purpose among the team. Their leadership wasn't just about their technical knowledge and climbing skills but more about fostering collaboration, safety, and confidence. By engaging with us closely, informing us, asking questions, and preparing us for the challenges ahead, they made the journey as much about mutual support as about reaching the summit. They provided a perfect example of what authentic engagement looks like in leadership.

Throughout my experiences of observing and listening to leaders, one of the most common things I have heard them say is, "I wish our employees cared more. If employees cared more about the company, its customers, and their work, there would be fewer problems." It's easy to understand this sentiment because, in essence, they're saying they wish their employees were more engaged, and as noted, that number is only slightly above thirty percent. This point of view has driven the growing interest among many organizations to measure employee engagement and take action to increase it, and leadership plays a critical role in doing so.

I am a former owner and operator of a small family restaurant, Big Daddy's Pizza in Central Ohio, so I understand the challenges of getting the most out of your staff—especially when most of them are high school and college students. It would be easy to assume these young employees were just there for a paycheck, and while that was often true, our expectations were simple: show up on time, stay safe, smile for the customers, do a good job, and get paid.

However, we were pleasantly surprised to find that many of them responded positively when given the chance to be more involved in the business. While a few showed little interest, most were eager to contribute to our success. Several became quite skilled at "running the shop," as we used to say. My wife and I encouraged this participation, not only because it was the right thing to do, but because it made good business sense. It allowed us to step away from the restaurant with confidence, knowing our staff could handle things in our absence—something any small business owner understands isn't easy.

All leaders wish their teams were fully engaged in their work. As statistics show, there's a direct correlation between engagement and key business outcomes like retention, customer satisfaction, and productivity. This has driven the growing interest in understanding how employees feel about their company, its leadership, and their work experience. At Big Daddy's Pizza, long before the term "employee engagement" existed, we recognized its importance, even if we didn't have a name for it.

Today, business leaders are increasingly focused on engagement alongside diversity, inclusion, and employee well-being. At their core, these efforts are about engaging the entire workforce. Engagement is more critical than ever in the business world.

We should commend leadership teams that analyze engagement data and seek to improve it. But reflecting on the Elevated Leaders I've known, I'd caution against overthinking engagement. The concept is simple: It's about doing something important together, working together as a team, tackling challenges as equals, with a shared sense of purpose and belonging. It means having the opportunity to do meaningful work in a positive environment and feeling valued for one's contributions.

Being engaged means truly feeling what it means to be "in this together," facing challenges as a united team with a common purpose. Elevated Leaders take ownership, build trust by holding themselves and others accountable, and eagerly engage with those who share a stake in success. They are passionate about their work and committed to their performance.

I think author Liz Wiseman managed to strike a deeper chord regarding engagement and its impact on performance in her fascinating book, *Multipliers*:

> Multipliers are leaders who look beyond their own genius and focus their energy on extracting and extending the genius of others. These are not "feel good" leaders. They are tough and exacting managers who see a lot of capacity in others and want to utilize that potential to the fullest.

This is a good explanation of why engagement is so critical. It is the only way to tap into what I would call the 'leadership' capacity of the organization. It also causes me to reflect on another Elevated Leader I had the privilege of meeting and working with while leading an organizational excellence assessment of a local hospital in my area. I'll call her Amanda, the CEO and chief medical officer for City General Hospital.

It's All for the Kids

When the assessment team arrived at the hospital for our official site visit, Amanda greeted each of us with a big enthusiastic smile and warm handshake. It had been six months since our first kick-off meeting, but she managed to remember each of our names.

"Welcome back Ali, Denise, Tim, Bengi, Tatum, Mark. I have to tell you, a lot has happened since your last visit." She was obviously referring to the groundbreaking of the new children's wing just two weeks before.

Amanda had recently taken over as CEO and Head Nurse after Dr. James, her predecessor, resigned. She was eager to get things started. James had been an incredible leader, and Amanda had big shoes to fill, but she was determined to take the hospital to new heights of community-based healthcare. Dr. James recommended her as his successor, recognizing her extraordinary career serving City General for many years first as a registered nurse, then executive administrator, and chief medical officer. Amanda's leadership and vision for the hospital was to create the best experience possible for patients and their families, and her approach was to engage the entire workforce, the patients, their families, and the community that the hospital serves.

The hospital had always been proud of its heritage. In 1932, a small group of Catholic nuns began a mission to serve the poor and underprivileged children on the outskirts east of town. They aimed to support their families while receiving care. Over the years, the hospital had undergone many changes, however, the primary mission of serving the underprivileged members of the community had remained the same. It was the job of Amanda and her leadership team to continue that mission into the twenty-first century. She was intent on making it everyone's job.

During the introductory meeting in October, Amanda and her leadership team were in a difficult place regarding the morale of the staff. City General was a relatively small downtown hospital that had long outgrown its original building, and perhaps nowhere was this more obvious than within the children's wing of the hospital. Pressured to find space to accommodate an ever-growing number of child patients, the staff and families were under stress, which, most importantly, created a negative patient experience.

Moreover, the leadership team had just received the latest staff engagement survey results, which were not good. Engagement was at the lowest it had ever been. This news was not a big surprise, as it was no secret that the hospital was overcrowded, understaffed, and using outdated equipment and technology. Additionally, the team had recently lost their beloved leader. Although many staffers respected and admired Amanda, it would be some time before they had the same level of trust or confidence in Amanda and her team. Trust needed to be earned; to do that, Amanda's team needed to take action to improve the situation at City Gen, and she saw the organizational assessment, conducted by an objective third party as a means of identifying their strengths, opportunities for improvement and recommendations for moving forward.

We sat around the table discussing the process we would use for the organizational assessment. Amanda was obviously ready to take on this challenge. She saw it as the perfect response to the engagement survey results. She sat back in her chair, slouching slightly with her fingers intertwined, and then she said, "You know, I don't think any of this is rocket science. People are asking for change. They wonder if the leadership team was hearing or taking their concerns seriously. They have a right to be engaged in all we do to whatever extent they can. Patients and their families said they liked the staff and the level of care and concern they received yet are undoubtedly aware of our inability to extend the type of care we would like to the families. As I always say, we must remind ourselves *it's all about the kids*. If we focus on that, we will all meet our mission. That is why I believe in this assessment process. It will provide us with a thoroughly objective measure against the best of the best. Let's not delude ourselves. We expect to score low, but we will know what to do to reach world-class healthcare status."

She returned to her seat and leaned over the table to view the materials again, then she raised her eyes and removed her reading glasses. "Quite simply, I believe everyone in this hospital, from the doctors to the nurses, the aids, technicians, and janitors, truly wants to provide what is best for the kids and their families. Furthermore," she added, "I know that many of our people have some great ideas of their own when it comes to how we do this. I know this to be true because they tell me." She cleared her throat before flashing a smile. "One thing I know to be true about our staff is that they truly care and are not shy about sharing their opinions and ideas."

She then sat back in her chair and gestured toward me and the team, "Well, my friends and colleagues, what do you say we get this thing moving?"

I was left speechless after hearing Amanda's persuasive argument for investing in the process. Her leadership was extraordinary, and it was a historic moment for the ninety-seven-year-old hospital and its entire staff. Amanda was fearless and determined to make the changes that were necessary to revive the old hospital in the city. She saw an opportunity to reimagine the hospital's original vision and mission and create a modern hospital for the future.

As planned, six months after our initial visit, our assessment team received the complete application from City General Hospital. During our review of the application, we were all impressed by the progress since our first meeting. It was clear that Amanda had followed through on her promise to engage everyone invested in the hospital's success. Immediately after our visit, Amanda and the leadership team began seeking input from patients and their families—those who could truly share the hospital experience and suggest improvements. They used short, engaging methods to gather feedback from children, allowing them to contribute ideas to make the hospital better for themselves and others. Next, Amanda involved the entire staff in planning and building the new children's wing. She organized focus groups within each hospital unit to provide valuable input to the architects and builders. This collaboration ensured that the final design reflected the needs and ideas of those who would use the space daily. Additionally, the team made a concerted effort to reach out to the community, keeping neighbors and the city informed of the hospital's plans and progress. They invited input on how the hospital could be a better neighbor and partnered with key community leaders, local political figures, and the city's mayor to strengthen these efforts. After reviewing these efforts and initiatives that had taken place since our last visit, one thing was certain: our assessment team and I were eager to see the progress that had been made during the official site-visit coming up in April.

As we arrived at the hospital for the official site visit, it was clear that construction was in full swing. A significant portion of the old parking lot was now a bustling construction zone, with architects and crews hard at work laying the foundation. As we looked up, a giant blue banner caught our eye, boldly proclaiming, in colorful letters, "It's All for the Kids"—Amanda's favorite mantra. I gently nudged Denise and pointed it out, and she smiled in response. We knew then that this site visit would be something special.

The visit officially began with the welcome meeting, where the assessment team outlined the agenda for the next three days: over 20 interviews, brief huddles with Dr. Kumar and the internal assessment team, and an executive briefing with Amanda and her team to wrap up the visit with a summary of the next steps. After this meeting, we split into pairs and began conducting interviews with employees representing various departments of the hospital. What we discovered was remarkable. Throughout the hospital, it was clear that Amanda had truly delivered on her promise to involve the entire staff in the construction of the new children's wing.

As we toured the hospital, we noticed vibrant banners on every floor, each depicting staff interacting with patients, families, and the community. The most striking images showed doctors, nurses, and technicians actively consulting with architects, builders, and interior designers.

These visuals told a powerful story, but the stories we heard during our interviews were even more impressive. Over the next three days, we validated the written responses from the organizational application and listened to countless tales of how each staff member had been deeply engaged in the hospital's development. It was the most extraordinary example of engagement I had ever witnessed.

When all the data was in and our assessment team completed our consensus review, City General scored highly, leading to the recommendation for a Gold Level Achievement of Excellence Award. The next time we saw Amanda and many of her staff was at the annual Excellence Award Conference, where it was an honor to watch them receive that well-deserved recognition. I couldn't help but reflect on what an incredible leader Amanda is—a true Elevated Leader who maximized her staff's potential through the power of engagement. Equally impressive was the level of engagement we observed from every single staff member we spoke to. Time and again, employees demonstrated genuine concern for the progress of the new children's wing, often going above and beyond their day-to-day duties to contribute to its success. It was clear that it was "all about the kids," and the actions of the staff spoke volumes—far more than any banner on the wall ever could.

CHAPTER NINE

Challenge

Challenge those you lead by setting high expectations, questioning the status quo, seeking improvement of both people and processes, exploring possibilities, and constantly raising expectations to inspire innovation, growth, and development.

Challenging employees is crucial for maintaining their engagement, motivation, and continuous growth. Organizations that do not provide meaningful challenges often find their employees feeling bored and stagnant, leading to a lack of motivation. This disengagement can significantly reduce productivity and increase turnover rates, and as employees seek more stimulating opportunities elsewhere, drive up recruitment and training costs.

The element of Challenge is about pushing individuals beyond their comfort zones and encouraging them to reach new heights. Elevated leaders recognize that growth and innovation occur when people are faced with new and demanding tasks. By setting high expectations and encouraging risk-taking, they create an environment where employees are motivated to learn, adapt, and excel. However, challenging others isn't about overwhelming them with unrealistic demands; it's about providing the right balance of support and autonomy so they can rise to the occasion.

In today's fast-paced and ever-evolving business landscape, the ability to adapt and innovate is crucial. Elevated Leaders understand this and prioritize creating a culture where challenges are seen as opportunities for growth, both for individuals and the organization as a whole. Whether through stretch assignments, cross-functional projects, or continuous learning opportunities, they ensure that their teams are always moving forward, equipped with the skills and resilience needed to tackle whatever comes their way.

Ultimately, challenging others is about fostering a mindset of continuous improvement and resilience. By embracing the element of Challenge, Elevated Leaders cultivate a culture of innovation, adaptability, and excellence, where every team member is encouraged to push their boundaries, take calculated risks, and contribute to the organization's long-term success.

Why do people climb mountains?

It's a question that every mountaineer—from the greenest beginner to the most seasoned veteran—answers the same way: because they are there. A big, bold challenge stares you in the face, daring you: *Come on, see what life is like up here. I dare you.*

As I write these words, I'm transported back to a moment twenty-five years ago, standing on the slopes of Mt. Rainier one evening after work. I was searching for something new and different, only to be met with a challenge from the most unexpected source.

It was then that I made a promise to myself: One day, I will return to climb Mt. Rainier's summit. Eighteen years later, I kept that promise. Though I fell just short of my goal—eleven hundred feet to be exact—that challenge revealed a part of myself I might never have discovered otherwise. The lesson was simple: The real value lies not in reaching the summit but in the challenge of setting and striving toward the goal.

That's why people climb mountains. Now, let me ask you: What mountain are you and your team trying to climb? What is your summit? How can you improve as a team? What do you want to see when you arrive? Consider how you can challenge yourself and others to reach higher.

The Center Wing

Little did I know how different this particular Monday morning would be as I sipped my hot coffee, trying to warm up on my drive to work. Upon arriving, I found a good parking spot and made my way into the plant, trudging through the ice and snow on a brisk 16-degree February morning. As team leader, I was to arrive thirty minutes before the start of my shift. I am glad I did.

As soon as I removed a couple of layers of clothes, I caught George, our group leader, headed in my direction. George was a good man, always jovial, upbeat, and energetic, despite his years of experience in the aerospace industry. I always enjoyed listening to his stories from back in the heyday when this same U.S. Navy-owned aerospace manufacturing plant was churning out hundreds of airplanes a month to support WWII, the Korean War, and the Vietnam War.

However, as George grew nearer, I could tell by the look on his face that he had something important on his mind. That smile was still on his face, but it was the sort of smile had something coming behind it.

He called me by my nickname. "Hey Moon, good morning to you," he said as he reached out his hand.

I gave it a shake. "Hi, boss, good morning," I replied. "What's going on? You're out and about bright and early."

"Ah, I just wanted to give you a heads up. You'll have a special visitor this morning at your team meeting."

"Oh, really? I don't suppose that special guest might be you?" I queried.

George smiled and said, "Well. I suppose so if you consider me special."

"Of course, you're special, George, in your own way," I said, poking him with a smile.

"Well, thank you, but I wasn't me I was referring to."

I looked at him, more surprised, "OK, then, who is this mystery guest?"

"Jim will be stopping by with a little challenge for you and your team."

Again, my interest was piqued. "That's it? Is that all you're going to tell me?

He grinned and slapped his hand on my shoulder. "I don't want to steal Jim's thunder. He's been working on this for some time. Don't fret. Your team is doing extremely well. Consider this a good sign that Jim likes what he sees in your team."

I would be lying if I said that I wasn't more than a little nervous as I sipped my coffee, greeting the rest of my team as they walked in the door: Big Red, Darla, Mike, Julie, JR, Barb, and Pete. Once everyone was seated in their customary places, I began. "Well, team, Happy Monday to you. You might want to grab a second cup of coffee this morning. We are going to have a special guest at our meeting."

That one got their attention, and they all looked up and straight at me.

Barb jumped in. "Oh, and who might that be?"

"Jim, the plant manager," I replied. "He should be here at seven-thirty following our regular team meeting."

"No shit?" Pete groused. "Now, what did we do wrong?"

I brushed him off. "Come on, Pete, why do you think we've done something wrong?"

Pete grumbled. "Well, why else would the plant manager take the time out of his day to attend our measly little team meeting?"

I knew Pete, and I understood where he was coming from. A dyed-in-the-wool UAW man, despite all of Jim's positive changes at the plant since his arrival, Pete was still suspicious of all "managers."

Big Red jumped in. "Hey, come on, Pete, lighten up a bit. It's not every day our plant's general manager comes to join our meeting." He tipped his coffee cup and took a few more sips before continuing, trying to get warm. Then he smiled beneath his bushy red beard. "I just hope he's bringing donuts."

Jim knocked on the door before Red could wipe that big grin off his face. We all turned to wave him in. He was a tall, rather lanky man, and he entered the room greeting everyone with a smile, handshakes, and a reserved, respectful nod. "Well, good morning, Team Phoenix!" he said with a sigh, having seen our corny team banner hanging across the door on his way in.

He received a hearty reply from most in the room and some grunting sound from Pete that sounded vaguely like "Mornin', boss."

Jim took the empty seat between Big Red and Darla. "Thank you for letting me be a part of your morning ritual here," he said with a smile.

"We're happy to have you, Jim. You're welcome to stop by anytime, as long as you bring the donuts," Darla quipped. She was returning with a full mug, and she set it on the table in front.

He laughed. "Yeah, I've noticed that a dozen donuts are a ticket through many doors around here. Anyway, I'm sure you're all wondering why I stopped by for coffee this morning, so let's get right to it."

I could tell he was a hardworking man who loved his work. He stood up and unrolled the blueprint he had kept stashed under his arm and rolled it open on the table, anchoring the corners with a couple of coffee mugs and the salt and pepper shakers.

"Well, team, I want to introduce you to the Center Wing Fuselage," he announced. He pointed to the blueprint of the sub-assembly. "Currently, this sub is being assembled at our sister plant in Salt Lake.

"I am sharing this with you this morning because this sub-assembly has proved to be a real headache for the folks out there. Most of the issues they have with it come down to the fact that nearly the entire assembly is titanium, which has given them fits when it comes to all the power-feed drilling sequences and otherwise highly tight tolerances in tight, difficult places."

As he explained the situation, he pointed to several places on the blueprint, pinpointing where these issues typically occurred. "They just don't have the equipment or operators needed to turn this around. It seems they have a significant turnover problem. They are losing workers as fast as they can train them. As a result, this assembly has been causing real issues, with numerous delays and slow tool turnaround times. These have now started to affect the overall ship schedule, which is lagging by two or almost three shipsets."

He picked up his mug, took a sip of coffee, and paced back and forth in the small confines of our team room. He went on. "For this reason, the program managers are looking for help in crashing the schedule. They plan to do so by finding a sister plant with the capacity and capability to start a second assembly station in hopes that we can get this thing back on track."

He paused, took a seat, and eyed the room as he leaned back in his chair. His chin tucked into his chest as he gazed up over his reading glasses. He looked around the table. "I know this team could do much better. Since the opening of this plant, Team Phoenix has been performing at a very high level. You have been tackling some of the most challenging assemblies in the entire plant. Every one of these assemblies requires some complicated operations, which is a testament to your knowledge, skills, and work ethic. When I got a call from St. Louis about possibly taking on this new challenge, I did not hesitate to recommend Team Columbus and Team Phoenix.

"So, let me get right to the point. I am here to ask this team to take on this new challenge. In four weeks, April twenty-third to be exact, we will begin this work; in fact, the tooling is already on its way here and should arrive sometime next week. It will occupy the space across the aisle from the Leading-Edge Wing assembly in your work cell." Jim paused once again, then he took a seat and another sip of his coffee. Then continued. "The current turnaround time is thirty-three days. It was originally twenty-six days, so you can see why these problems are starting to hamper our schedule. The plan is for your team to take three of six shipsets off their hands so we can get the schedule back on track, but here's the catch: This is in addition to keeping the Leading-Edge Wing assemblies on track or ahead of schedule," he said, pointing out to the shop floor.

Jim looked across the table to our Group Leader. "George and I have worked out a plan to transfer three mechanics from Eagle Team No. 3 to your team. They can help in any way you need them, but they are not certified power-feed drill operators. This will free up three or perhaps four to tackle this challenge.

"Aside from that, how you get this done is entirely up to your team. You have taken on some tough jobs, so this is no different. My money is on this team. This is a chance for this team and our plant to show headquarters what is possible here at the Columbus plant." Jim paused for effect as he gazed around the room, and for some reason, he fixed his final gaze on me. Then went on. "I have sold my bosses on the idea that we are prepared to take on the entire assembly schedule. You will work with George here to work out a production plan. If there is anything that you need from me or George, let us know. This will become the top priority. I'll be back in a couple of weeks to see what you've come up with."

Again, there was a slight pause as he gazed up over his readers again. "They are doing this in thirty-three days. I believe you can turn these around in thirty days or less. I know you're up to the challenge. Once again, thanks for the coffee. Now I got to get back to work."

That's when Pete chimed in. Seemingly more alive and certainly more audible. "Whaddaya mean, Jim? I thought this was work." Chiding him a little.

Jim laughed. "Oh no, Pete, this stuff isn't work—this is fun. What's waiting for me back in my office is work."

Pete laughed and nodded. I was so pleased to see Pete come alive that morning. Jim's challenge in front of us seemed precisely what he needed to become more engaged.

Later, Pete confided in me that he was buying in a little more. He would withhold judgment until he saw real action from management. "I've seen it before—much hype in the beginning, but then same old BS when things get serious."

Jim was back, as promised, two weeks to the day. This Monday, however, showed signs of promise. The weather had taken a turn toward spring, with seventy-degree temperatures and a nice breeze blowing in through the high bay doors. The faint, sweet smell of jet fuel wafted in now and then from the Port Columbus Airport runway next door.

The team was ready. We had set aside extra time in our meetings to analyze the job and the work involved. George, our team leader, along with Melody and Kevin, the two engineers assigned to the task, joined us. As the team leader, I was humbled by the incredible expertise of our mechanics and the collaboration with the engineers. It was teamwork at its finest as they discussed the best approach, equipped with an arsenal of power-feed drills. However, the task was far from simple. Even the smallest holes had to be drilled by hand, requiring incredibly tight tolerances. The material was tough—much more challenging than working with soft aluminum—and the work had to be done in a relatively small space.

The key was figuring out the best sequence of steps and timing them precisely to achieve the most efficient operation. Once that was determined, it was just a matter of execution, and I had complete confidence in my team's ability to get the job done.

I led the explanation of our plan, pointing to some diagrams and numbers that we had scribed on the whiteboard. Jim sat there without saying a word and other team members chimed in where needed. "We got to the final time estimate once we reviewed all the plan details," I explained. "Jim, we believe we can turn this around in twenty-six or maybe twenty-five days, which is conservative."

Jim sat there and pondered it all. He sat in silence for what seemed an eternity. Then he spoke up. "I think it's a great plan. I can see it. I can understand it. Now, we need to make it happen."

Without hesitation, every person around the room nodded. It was obvious that Jim had everyone's attention. Suddenly, there was a lot more riding on this experiment than we realized. Word got around the plant fast that if we were successful with this plan, it could mean all the work would be coming our way. I did like feeling a little pressure, but I was confident in what the team had come up with. I was what you might call a novice mechanic at the time, and this is why they likely chose me to be their team leader: simply to keep me out of the way. I was totally fine with that.

The team was energized and determined. We brought on Tony, Geoff, and Emily from the trailing edge team, and they were excellent mechanics; this allowed Big Red, Pete, and Barb to focus primarily on staffing the power-feed drills around the clock while Julie and I joined the others to focus on the leading-edge assembly.

During the weeks following our team meeting, we gained an entirely new purpose. We gathered each morning to check our production plan and to use the knowledge we had gained as part of our training in Total Quality Management and Lean practices. Not only was it fascinating to see the results of our efforts, but it was also rather extraordinary to see how the same team of people can be transformed when given a challenge.

Our team delivered the first assembly in twenty-six days, exactly as planned. Even more impressively, with the engineers' help, the team had already begun refining workflows, which reduced our lead time. The next assembly was completed in twenty-four days, and the third in just twenty-one days—six days ahead of our plan and twelve days faster than anything Salt Lake could achieve. Our strong performance led to the decision to send more shipsets our way until we took on the entire workload. It was a huge victory for our assembly Team Phoenix and our entire Team Columbus facility.

The week before we started loading Ship No. 18 into the tool—the first of all assemblies that were now being built at Team Columbus—Jim stopped by our meeting. He was wearing jeans, a hunting vest, and a cowboy hat, a side of him that people knew about but rarely saw. He knocked on the door. We all waved him in. He removed his hat before stepping through the door.

Once inside, Jim immediately apologized. "Hello everyone, sorry for all the get-up here. I was just headed out for one of our big horse shows.

If you didn't know, my wife and I show our horses. We have a big show going on downtown at the fairgrounds." Then he stepped in further, hat in hand. "I don't want to take too much of your time, I just wanted to stop by today to say thanks for taking on that challenge. I must admit, the way this team responded really made me proud. It also made it much easier for me to convince my bosses that the entire job should come to us. You made us all proud." He paused as he put on his riding hat, then ended his visit by saying, "Now, it looks like we have a lot of work to do, but first, I got some horses I have to show."

Jim turned, stepped out of the door, and went on his way, like the hero riding off into the sunset, but it was apparent who the real heroes were. I know I was walking on air after all that. I was just so proud to be part of a truly high-performing team, and we, quite literally, won the battle.

Jim, our GM and COO, was a true Elevated Leader, a master in the art of Challenge. He had the wisdom to recognize the potential in his people—often before we saw it in ourselves—and used significant challenges to galvanize the team and the entire workforce. Like mountaineers who understand that it's not just about reaching the summit but about working together as a team to meet the challenge and ensuring everyone grows from the experience.

As Ralph Waldo Emerson wisely said, "It's not the destination; it's the journey."

CHAPTER TEN

Coach

The growth is in the journey. Coach those you lead by providing the right direction and support as they strive to meet these challenges. Coaches ensure psychological safety for others when they are being pushed outside of their comfort zone.

Coaching is a vital element of employee development and organizational success. When employees do not receive coaching, they are less likely to meet their performance goals, which can lead to disengagement and stagnation. In contrast, employees who receive coaching often experience improved work performance and greater job satisfaction. Without coaching, organizations may face lower engagement, decreased productivity, and higher turnover rates, leading to significant costs in terms of lost talent and resources.

The element called Coach involves more than just giving feedback; it's about guiding, mentoring, and developing others to reach their full potential. Elevated Leaders understand that effective coaching is a continuous process that requires patience, empathy, and a deep commitment to the growth of others. By actively listening, providing constructive feedback, and helping individuals set and achieve meaningful goals, they create an environment where everyone feels supported and motivated to excel.

In today's competitive and dynamic work environment, coaching is essential for building high-performing teams and fostering a culture of continuous improvement. Elevated Leaders prioritize coaching as a key strategy for unlocking potential and driving performance. Whether through one-on-one mentoring, structured development programs, or regular performance reviews, they ensure that their team members have the guidance and support needed to navigate challenges, develop new skills, and achieve their goals.

Ultimately, coaching is about investing in the long-term success of individuals and the organization. By embracing the element Coach, Elevated Leaders create a culture of growth, accountability, and excellence, where every team member is empowered to reach their highest potential and contribute meaningfully to the organization's success.

Disappointment Cleaver

The Disappointment Cleaver (DC) route to the summit of Mount Rainier is the most popular path to the top. Seventy-five percent of all summit attempts are made via "The DC," making it one of the most guided routes in North America.

It is also considered the easiest route; however, our guides had warned us about a particularly tough section of the route that would be even more challenging due to the unusually warm temperatures that summer, which left little snow cover. I quickly learned what that meant. When climbing on the DC, especially with crampons, it's ideal to have a nice blanket of ice and snow beneath your feet. Instead, we faced a staircase of bare, jagged rocks scattered down the mountainside by an ancient eruption.

The route's name felt eerily fitting for me and my pursuit. After about an hour of climbing this stairway to oblivion, I was holding my own, thanks to my better-than-average fitness. Yet, as I had feared, I started noticing a subtle weakness on my left side, particularly in my ankle—a vulnerability that revealed itself at the worst possible time. The strenuous hike in the dark of the early morning was taxing, but somehow, I pushed through, making it to our next break atop a glacial ridge.

After about an hour and a half of climbing we finally reached a spot aptly named High Break, which was, according to Gregg, the spot for our respite. "Alright, everyone, let's get some food and water. This will be our last stop before we attempt the summit. How's everyone doing?" he asked. The response was muted, as the entire group tried to recover from the last round of Rainier's relentless challenges.

"We will rest for twenty minutes," he announced. "We'll be around to check in on everyone."

In the wee hours of the morning just 1,100 feet from the summit, I sank onto my backpack, utterly exhausted but still eager to continue. Looking up at the night sky, I saw a dome of stars stretching in every direction, from one horizon to the other. It was a moonless night, and I could see the lights of Tacoma and Seattle in the distance, framing Rainier's sister peaks in the Tahoma Range.

As I sat there, I felt like I was having an out-of-body experience, floating above the world, contemplating my place in it. The only thought that came to mind was of my wife, waiting alone at the hotel while I was 13,000 feet above her, chasing a crazy dream.

My reflection was interrupted by the sound of boots crunching on the snow. I turned to see KM, one of the mountain guides who had been with me most of the way, coming over to check on me.

"Hey, buddy, how are you doing?" he asked in his thick Austrian accent as he took a seat beside me.

"I'm doing all right," I replied, half-heartedly, beginning to feel some doubt creeping in. "That was pretty rough," I admitted.

KM nodded. "Yes, it was rough for everyone. Those rocks were no fun. That's why we're checking in with everyone." He paused briefly. "I noticed you had a couple of stumbles on the way up," he said.

I nodded. "Yes, like I said, it was rough."

KM continued. "I'm bringing this up because you mentioned the weakness in your ankle back at Camp Muir. I'm guessing it's starting to become a real problem."

I nodded again. "Yeah, I think so, but I still think I'll be alright." I resisted the idea that it might be time to turn back.

KM sat in silence with me for a few moments, then spoke again. "Listen, my friend, I have no doubt that you're fit enough to reach the summit. That's not my concern. But it doesn't get any easier on the descent, especially when exhaustion hits. I can't recommend that you continue."

I nodded, reluctantly. "So, do I have a choice?"

"Yes, it is your choice," he said, "but you need to consider that I'm preparing to lead some others back to Camp Muir, and this is the last chance to turn back. From here on, there's no turning back."

I pondered his words, reflecting on everything that had brought me this far—just 1,100 feet from my goal. Then I corrected myself. The goal was to attempt the summit and return safely. Once again, the thought of my wife and family waiting below came to mind. Finally, I looked KM in the eye and nodded one last time. I swallowed a lump in my throat and replied, "Yes, I agree."

KM gave me a few seconds to process everything, then spoke up.

"Hey, I know it's never easy to fall short of the summit. If it makes you feel any better, only fifty-eight percent of those who make the attempt actually reach it, so you are not alone. You've been very impressive for a first-time climber but it is our job to get you back safely." Then he patted his huge, gloved hand on my knee. "Hey, besides, I could use your help on the way down."

This surprised me. Based on our conversation, how in the world could I be of any assistance now?

"Uh-oh! What exactly does that mean?" I asked quizzically.

"Well, it's you and me, and Alberto, who is sick as a dog and leaving his mountain breakfast on the glacier. Then there's his brother Jesus, who has apparently bummed his knee by the way he is walking, and then our friend Hitomi, who is just plain exhausted and probably undernourished. So, if I had to pick someone from this group to take up the rear on our descent, I would pick you."

I sat there somewhat dumbfounded by what I just heard, but it made all the sense in the world now that the paradigm had changed. Indeed, I was the right pick, but all I could think about was, *if I am the right choice, how bad off is the field of likely candidates?*

KM persisted. "Watch, listen, and follow my orders, and you will be fine. I need you to keep an eye on the rest of the team to see how they are doing. We have about a four-hour hike back down to Camp Muir. It's tough at first, as you well know, to go back down the Cleaver. After that, the descent gets easier. Not easy, but easier. We will take as many breaks as you and I think we need. There is no rush; think safety first. Got it?"

I nodded my head again. "Got it."

KM stood up. "Alrighty then, we head out in fifteen minutes."

On the way down to Camp Muir, the team faced several challenges as we descended Disappointment Cleaver on the rope. Albert was in second position, followed by his brother Jesus, Hitomi, and me at the rear. After about ninety minutes of descending, it was clear that Hitomi was having a tough time, barely trudging along. Then suddenly, he stumbled badly, Fortunately, he fell directly forward about three feet. I felt the pull on the rope but managed to hold firm with Jesus's help. I called out to KM. "Hold, KM, I think we need a break."

KM had already turned his attention back to Hitomi. "No problem. Let's take a few minutes here," he replied, checking him for any injuries. "Keep your packs on but take some weight off your feet for a while." As we rested, I thought to myself, *What a motley crew we are*. It became apparent that Alberto was still suffering from stomach cramps caused by diarrhea. Meanwhile, Jesus was pushing through despite his hamstring troubles. He was sitting, rubbing his right knee.

KM checked on everyone else, staying positive and encouraging us all to stay focused. "We are nearly through the toughest part. We will take a longer break in about an hour. If you're feeling the need to rest, we rest."

Hitomi seemed more energized after a brief rest. His little fall had been a wake-up call. When I asked if he was ready to continue, he nodded. "Yes, I am OK," he said in his best English.

KM patted him on the head and said, "OK, Hitomi, let us know if you need to stop for a rest. There's no need to push yourself too much." Hitomi nodded again, more alert and confident, which gave me a sense of relief. We were all reminded of the dangers we faced and how much we depended on each other.

We continued down the mountain for another hour or so, finally leaving The Cleaver behind. By the time we reached our next long break, we were beyond exhaustion but feeling better, knowing we'd soon be walking on snow and ice instead of the unforgiving volcanic rock.

KM came over to check on me. "Hey, buddy, how are *you* doing?"

I smiled, nodding confidently. "I'm doing good. I think I'm starting to get the hang of this mountain guide thing."

"I'm glad to hear that," he chuckled. "but we're not done yet. Our climbing companions are struggling. Please keep doing what you're doing and watch the climbers in front of you. Hitomi is improving, but Alberto is not doing well. The next section won't be too difficult, but we'll cross a glacier with cracks and crevasses. We'll be moving slowly, and I'll check in every ten to fifteen minutes. Clear?"

"Yeah, I've got it," I said, though my confidence wavered.

He patted my arm. "Listen, what you're doing right now is more important than reaching the summit. We all get back safely, right?"

"Yep, that's right. Just let me know when you're ready to head out," I replied, feeling a renewed sense of purpose.

I never imagined my trip up Mt. Rainier would end the way it did, but I'm grateful for the experience. I learned a lot about myself once I was placed in a critical position to help ensure we all made it back unharmed. I was thankful that KM had put his trust in me.

An Elevated Leader understands that when we are empowered to take on a challenge, we must meet it with the right balance of coaching, support, and direction. Reflecting on that trip down Disappointment Cleaver, KM provided a perfect example of an Elevated Leader demonstrating the core element Coach. He maintained my sense of purpose and contribution to the team, even when I fell short of a personal goal, by showing concern and offering just the right amount of guidance and support when I needed it most.

Pursuing Excellence

One of my most memorable encounters with an Elevated Leader happened during a benchmarking visit as part of my company's Quest for Excellence (QE) team. As a QE organization, Harris Manufacturing (HM) often had the opportunity to visit other member organizations to observe, study, and exchange best practices, all in the spirit of continuous improvement.

These visits were quite involved, following specific steps and guidelines to ensure actionable insights for both teams. Typically, visiting team members would spend one or two days on-site before hosting a reciprocal visit a few weeks later.

One such benchmarking exchange took place between HM and another manufacturing firm across the state. I had arranged the visits with Sandy, my counterpart from EX Performance, after meeting her at the State Quest for Excellence conference the previous year. We scheduled the first benchmarking visit for October, with EXP graciously offering to host.

Although both of our companies were in manufacturing, our products and operations couldn't have been more different. We produced mission-critical pressure relief valves for nuclear, fossil fuel, and chemical processing plants, while our benchmarking partners specialized in high-pressure hoses, valves, and fittings for high-performance automobiles. These differences were exactly why we chose to benchmark with them—innovation often springs from those who operate outside the familiar boundaries of product, customer base, machinery, methods, and processes.

Upon our arrival at the plant, Sandy was the first to greet us in the lobby. Her bold, friendly, and outgoing personality matched her robust and sturdy frame. She welcomed us with a hearty "Well, welcome, everyone! So glad to meet you!" and eagerly reached out to shake hands.

After introductions, Sandy directed us to collect our badges at the front desk. Once officially registered, she led us through the front door and to a large room where the rest of her team awaited us, just in time for bagels and coffee.

A few minutes later, with bagels and coffee in hand, Sandy stood up to take charge. "Good morning, everyone!" she called out, clasping her hands together.

The response was lukewarm.

"Ah, come on now! GOOD MORNIN', everyone!" she boomed, this time commanding our full attention.

She nodded, satisfied. "Alrighty then, that's much better," she said with a smile. "I think some of us might need a little more coffee."

She quickly organized us and prepared us for the tasks ahead, dividing the group into two teams of eight, each team with four members. Team A, led by Sandy, focused on the operational aspects of the study. I was part of Team B, which concentrated on the people and culture aspects.

Sandy's team included Bo, the quality assurance team lead from EXP; Al, HM's director of manufacturing; and Sunjay, HM's engineering manager. My team included Annette, a production coordinator; Steve, a manufacturing engineer from EXP; Donna, HM's procurement manager; and Frank, our general manager at HM.

We set out to divide and conquer after receiving our materials and agenda for the day. We were scheduled to meet back in the conference room at 2:30 p.m. for our first debrief. Sandy led me and the others back to the manufacturing office, where she had prepared a conference table and space for a large whiteboard. As we stepped in, she pointed toward the whiteboard, which displayed a comprehensive graphic representation of everything that flowed through the plant—from receiving to shipping and everything in between. This was visually represented with numbers in tables, various symbolic geometric shapes, and smaller diagrams showing even more detail of the work that flows through each work cell.

"This is our entire value stream," she said. "We have been working on this for months, with many of our shop floor employees contributing to mapping all of this out."

I continued to gaze at this work of art on her whiteboard, astounded. *Rack up the first big takeaway from our visit,* I thought. I had seen my fair share of value stream maps, but this one was exceptional. Even more impressive, Sandy was leading the charge to ensure the entire plant was focused on making continual improvements across the board. She explained how the map is used to identify opportunities for improvement in every work cell, eliminate wasted resources, and improve flow. It's no easy task with over 2,300 different part numbers produced every day.

"You know, when I started at this place, I was a production worker, and I always complained that many things just didn't make sense in the shop: how the work was managed, organized, and executed. It always seemed to me there was a better, faster, cheaper, and, quite frankly, easier way to do things. And that's what we are doing now: just giving people a chance to get engaged in making things better," she concluded with a shrug.

She then motioned for us to sit at the small conference table. Once we were seated, she continued. "This hasn't been easy by any means. Over the years, a lot of bad blood has flowed through this plant between employees, management, and two different unions. Cooperation on anything like this was almost unheard of."

I just sat and listened, nodding my head. When Sandy paused, Al posed the next question. "So, what has changed to make that happen?"

She explained, "Well, it's quite simple. We've more or less been told by our executive management to get our act together and get this plant performing at the level of our competitors, or there's going to be an easy decision about what to do with this aging plant. We have the highest costs and expenses of any of our key competitors. While they've been making great strides with their operations, cutting costs, and streamlining processes, we can't compete on price. Likewise, we've lost our advantage as the highest quality supplier because our competitors are now producing high-quality products as well. It comes down to making many small, incremental improvements across the entire value stream. That's the bottom line.

"This is the best job for miles around, and I know 927 employees who would like to keep their jobs, including myself. I'm not quite ready to go back to farming full-time." The plant was in a very rural, agricultural area, some seventy-five miles from the nearest modest-sized city.

I nodded again and sat back in my chair. "Well, I guess the benchmarking has begun," I said.

Sandy smiled, "Yes, I guess so." She pulled out the forms we used to take notes during the visit. I grabbed a pen and jotted down a few notes.

Then Al asked another question. "So, tell me, what have you and your team been doing to make this happen?"

She was quick with her answer. "Oh, that's easy. I think the biggest thing has been creating a 'coaching culture.' Sometimes, I think of myself and our implementation team as coaches, coaching our teams. As I said, we managed to surpass the biggest resistance points. Still, when it comes to identifying clear, achievable goals for improvement, making the necessary changes, and sustaining those changes, coaching has been the secret sauce. It certainly took some time to work through those points of resistance, and most everyone has been really engaged and quite excited to be a part of what we are trying to accomplish.

"Thanks to some help from corporate, we have spent, and continue to spend, a reasonable amount of time and money training our associates to learn these Lean techniques and methods. They have been great at putting them into practice. However, more was needed. To sustain those changes, you have to follow the training with on-site coaching, removing obstacles, encouraging the free exchange of ideas, and, most importantly, doing so in a way that demonstrates respect for what everyone brings to the table.

"I saw this as critical, so I petitioned Jeff, our plant manager, to let me take our team leaders and Lean Six Sigma Black Belts through a good coaching training program. It was really intense, and we learned so much. We teach them to use the GROW coaching model. I'm sure you must have heard of it. It stands for Goal, Reality, Options, and Will to Act." She recited each, counting them on her fingers to describe the model. "We all learned how to use this model when coaching each other and our teams.

"This was a real game changer because most of these folks, while they are great at making changes to the workplace, could be better at leading others through these changes. This makes all the difference in whether the changes can be made swiftly and successfully, and if they don't work, we try again."

She paused long enough to take a couple of sips of her coffee, then continued. "OK, in a couple of minutes, we are going to begin with a plant tour. It's actually great timing because it's the first week of the quarter, and it's time for what we call our Fall Sprint. A few chosen teams will shut down their production lines for up to three days to make any improvements they have identified that require interruptions to the process. While they're at it, they will also conduct their 5S process for workplace cleanliness and organization. I think you'll see that the folks really get into it."

After a quick break, we met Sandy in the cafeteria to begin the tour. Before doing so, she explained what was happening in more detail.

"As we make our way around the plant, we will stop at each work cell involved in our sprint. Each team has identified one or more incremental improvements they will implement. I say 'mostly' incremental in that one of those teams, Team Seven, is working on a big change to their work cell regarding improving the overall workflow. This involves moving heavier equipment, re-running the electricals, re-programming, etcetera."

"Wow!" Sunjay reacted, appreciating the extent of work Sandy was referring to. "That's a lot to complete in three days."

"Yeah," Sandy agreed. "It is a lot, but we have a great team of good people working on this. I plan to spend a couple of hours with them this afternoon so you can get a good look for benchmarking purposes." Sandy clasped her hands and said, "OK, let's get started."

During our visit to the plant, we went from one Kaizen team to the next. At each station, we took a few minutes to review the work cell's key performance indicators on the team's scorecard. The scorecard displayed various metrics such as cell productivity, lead times, delivery, efficiency, and quality. In addition, we tracked Kaizen improvements with a focus on the Fall Sprint.

At each stop, the team leaders spent time conversing with Sandy and our benchmarking team, explaining what was happening in the work cell regarding the improvements they were being challenged to make. I observed Sandy fully engaged with the team leaders and members, asking loads of questions, challenging assumptions, and, in many cases, pushing the teams to get the improvements in place.

In most cases, the teams knew exactly what they needed to get done and how to accomplish it. Sandy didn't interfere much but let them know she was there if they needed anything. In other cases, if the team or team members happened to be struggling, she would step in to provide as much direction and support as might be needed. For the most part, it was obvious that the Team Leaders and Black Belts were handling things flawlessly, also practiced in coaching individuals and teams through the process.

Later that afternoon, we made our way to Team Seven's work cell, and just as Sandy had promised, it was a beehive of activity. She explained that due to the amount of work taking place, this was an "extended" team, meaning that the regular team members were joined by two manufacturing engineers, CNC programmers, maintenance technicians, and three material handlers—all needed to make the type of workflow changes they were aiming for.

We spent two hours observing, listening in, and asking as many questions as possible without interrupting or getting in the way of progress. We mainly just observed. Seeing the level of engagement from every team member, focused intently on getting the job done, was amazing. However, what stood out again was how many of the team members collaborated and coached each other through the changes being implemented. The level of engagement was astounding. I had never seen anything like it in a manufacturing plant.

The tour continued as our two teams went their separate ways, spending the remainder of the day digging into more specifics regarding benchmarking activity. Eventually, we regrouped in the conference room again, around 4:00 p.m. that afternoon for the wrap-up meeting. We thanked Sandy and her team for being such wonderful hosts. Then we took some time to have each team share our lessons learned and the takeaway actions that we had agreed to. I had to admit to Sandy and her team that I felt some pangs of jealousy at what they were able to achieve over the past couple of years. Back home, we still had quite a way to go, but we learned a lot from the visit. Lastly, before we said our goodbyes, we scheduled a date for the next benchmarking meeting at our place.

On our way back to our plant that evening, our team was already comparing notes on what we felt were the most significant lessons from our visit. As was always the case, plenty of operational excellence lessons were to be learned and practices to be adopted. We were excited about the changes we were already preparing to make. However, we had one overriding takeaway. Frank, our general manager, summed it up best: "You know, there was just something different about that place. You could almost sense it as soon as you walked in the door. The culture was palpable."

We all agreed, nodding our heads. Then Donna added, "Yes, that is precisely what I would say, Frank. There was just something about it. It had much to do with Sandy's leadership and how she and her team built a coaching culture. People find it hard to make changes and sustain them, and she gets that. Hence, their investment in training people and creating those coaching skills."

Again, we all agreed.

"It wasn't just Sandy," Al interjected. He sat in the co-pilot's chair of our tiny mini-bus. "Obviously, she and the entire team have the full support of the leadership team. It's no small thing that they're shutting down production lines to do their Kaizen projects and investing time and money into their people. That takes the support of the company, but yes, I agree. The coaching was critical because corporate support can soon dwindle if you're not coming through as promised."

We all grew silent for a moment; then Frank, our GM, spoke up after taking a sip of his Coke. "Well, that all falls on me. I know we can do much better. Whatever this team thinks it needs to move our QE program forward, let me know. I'm sure I could use a little coaching myself." He tipped his Coke can and chugged what was left.

Elevated Leaders recognize the need to coach others as they pursue their goals. They know it's not enough to challenge someone to "strive for higher ground;" you must also be there to provide the right direction and support if the coachee is to learn and grow from the experience.

CHAPTER ELEVEN

Celebrate

Celebrate with those you lead, both successes and failures. Acknowledge the difference but recognize that both are equal in value when it comes to leadership development. However, these experiences are only something to celebrate with reflection and learning from that reflection.

Celebration and recognition are powerful drivers of employee engagement and retention. When employees feel unappreciated due to a lack of recognition and celebration, they are more likely to leave their jobs in search of environments where their contributions are valued. This not only increases recruitment and training costs but also disrupts team cohesion and continuity. Conversely, regular recognition and celebration can significantly boost morale, enhance engagement, and improve retention, fostering a more positive and productive workplace.

The element of Celebrate goes beyond merely acknowledging accomplishments; it's about creating a culture of appreciation and recognition. Elevated leaders understand that celebrating successes—both big and small—reinforces the behaviors and attitudes that contribute to the organization's goals. By recognizing individual and team achievements, they foster a sense of pride, belonging, and motivation among their team members, encouraging them to continue striving for excellence.

In today's fast-paced work environment, taking the time to celebrate milestones and successes is more important than ever. Elevated leaders prioritize celebration as a key element of their leadership approach, ensuring that their teams feel valued and appreciated. Whether through formal recognition programs, team celebrations, or simple expressions of gratitude, they make it a point to acknowledge and celebrate the hard work and dedication of their team members.

Ultimately, celebration is about building a positive and resilient organizational culture. By embracing the element of Celebrate, Elevated Leaders create an environment where every achievement is acknowledged, and every team member feels valued. This not only strengthens individual and team morale but also reinforces the collective commitment to the organization's long-term success.

Breakfast at Sunrise

KM, our guide, was true to his word. After a few challenging sections of the descent, trekking across snow and ice became much more straightforward than climbing rock in crampons. We were also starting to gain confidence as the light of sunrise began to fill the eastern sky, illuminating our path. The climbing team caught its second wind. Alberto was feeling much better and had eaten what he couldn't stomach earlier on the descent. Hitomi regained his composure and took more decisive steps. As for me, I was beyond exhaustion, but I felt a deep sense of accomplishment despite not having reached the summit.

We came upon a relatively flat, snow-covered plane on the glacier. Daylight was dawning as KM paused for a quick drink of water. We halted as he looked back at us.

"How's everyone doing?" he asked.

We all gave a nod and a thumbs up.

"We're going to make tracks across this stretch in front of us. I know a great place to take an extended break before we head down to Camp Muir."

Once again, we all gave a thumbs up, capped our water bottles, and set off across the glacier.

After about twenty-five minutes of easy trekking, the early traces of dawn became brighter, with neighboring peaks casting long, mysterious shadows across the glacier. We eventually arrived at another wall of ice, about thirty feet high, that had to be navigated via a narrow path before reaching an outcropping—a sort of open ledge carved out of the ice.

Just as we arrived, the entire area was illuminated by the sun's first light, now beginning to rise on the eastern horizon. There were several boulders of various shapes and sizes that made for excellent recliners.

"Well, what do you think? Pretty nice, huh?" KM asked as we all found spots to drop our packs and make ourselves comfortable.

We all turned to look at KM as he stood gazing into the distance. That's when it hit us. The entire eastern sky was cast in a brilliant red-orange glow, with Little Tahoma silhouetted in front. The early sunrise painted a breathtaking landscape. The east flank of Mt. Rainier was bathed in the same light, with patches of exposed ice glistening like diamonds partially buried in the snow. As the light struck the wall of ice behind us, it refracted into every color of the rainbow. It was stunningly beautiful—an experience I never dreamed I would have.

I wasn't alone in my awe; everyone in our entire motley crew of new friends and climbers stood transfixed, absorbing as much of the experience as possible. It wasn't easy, at least for me, to wrap my mind around what I saw. All I knew was that I was glad to be there.

KM broke the silence. "Not a bad place for a bite of breakfast. What do you say?"

"You did a great job, KM. Nice spot. Thanks!" I replied.

He smiled and nodded. Then he turned to sit on one of the boulders, digging into his pack, searching for something. Eventually, he pulled out a small half-pint bottle of Jack Daniels whiskey and held it up in the air. "I think it's time for a celebration."

KM noticed our surprised looks and flashed a big grin. "Oh, no worries, folks, it's just some nice, strong sweet tea. But hey, it's the thought that counts, right?"

We all laughed, relieved we weren't about to start sipping whiskey, not in the condition or situation we were in. It was a great gag, but more importantly, we appreciated the thoughtful, symbolic gesture behind it. KM had deliberately planted that little gag in his pack for just such a moment, just in case there was a good reason to celebrate—and now we had one.

He took a symbolic sip, playfully twisted his face, and then passed the little bottle over to me. I took a whiff.

KM laughed. "What's the matter? Don't you trust your trusty guide?"

Sure enough, there was no trace of alcohol. I smiled, lifted the little bottle, and took a couple of sips. Indeed, it was sweet tea—very, very strong tea. I passed the bottle to Hiroshi, who followed our lead. He took a sip, lifted the bottle again, and took another. He passed it along. We each took a few sips. It was very tasty and provided an excellent energy boost.

KM pointed toward the stunning scene unfolding in all its glory before us. "In case you're wondering, that's the Three Sisters," he said, pointing far off to the southeast at three dark blue silhouettes starkly contrasting against a blood-orange sky. "That's Faith, Hope, and Charity," he said, pointing to each in succession. He paused. "Yep, this is a fantastic shot for sure—most of the time, they are shrouded in morning clouds, but not today."

There were silent nods all around as we took in the view.

KM added, "And you know what? The summit party won't see this."

He grinned. We smiled.

He continued as he reclined against the glacier wall. "This was my twenty-first trip up this mountain, and I must tell you, not one is the same. Indeed, not every climber makes it to the summit. I've heard that only fifty-eight percent of those who attempt it actually reach the summit. So that means almost half of us fail from time to time. But look at what you would be missing if you hadn't tried. More importantly, as a guide, I recognize that the difference between a great experience and a not-so-great experience is all in how you look at it. The fact that we are here together now, in this amazing place, is reason enough to celebrate our experience together."

KM understood the importance of stopping to celebrate the occasion, and being afforded the opportunity to do so is why I'm writing about that celebration even today. I can't deny that I was heartbroken when I realized I wouldn't reach the summit. However, looking back, I wouldn't have traded the experience for anything else in the world, and much of that had to do with our amazing mountain guides—especially our trusty guide KM. Indeed, they were all Elevated Leaders. Hats off to those trusty mountain guides.

The Job

I felt honored and excited to be invited back again to Versitec—my third visit in the past year. I must have been doing something right.

During my previous visits, I conducted leadership workshops and on-site consulting to support the implementation of our company's operational excellence program. Fortunately, as a result, I established strong relationships with many of my colleagues there.

Versitec was a specialized safety valve maintenance and repair operation located in Louisiana. It was a proud company that built its reputation on its original owner's hard work and leadership legacy. Its speed, quality, and reputation for excellent customer service set it apart from competitors.

Working with the incredible team at Versitec was a delight. Even on the hottest summer days, drenched in sweat one minute and shivering in the air conditioning the next, it was the most excellent place one could be in the heart of Cajun country. As part of my visit, the team was eager to walk me through the shop to see the great work done with their 5S routines. The transformation was extraordinary. What had been a typical, dirty, grimy, greasy maintenance shop, with items stored here and there, with no regard for organization, was now an extremely clean and brightly lit shop with three distinct work cells. The team had cleaned and fully restored every piece of equipment to near-perfect working conditions. Each cell was lined with storage bins, labeled and clean, with tools, equipment, and supplies all organized by "POUFOU," as the folks called it. Locate the tools and supplies you need by Point of Use and Frequency of Use. It was all far from perfect, but it was night and day compared to what the shop looked like before.

Stepping out to the docking and staging area was much the same. Most notable was the new hoist and crane equipment, which provided much more flexibility when handling large and heavy assets. It also offered a broader stream of business, being the only repair shop that could handle such equipment. After my walk-through and lots of warm teasing from the folks in the shop, I assured them that they deserved a ten out ten in my mind, referring to the rating system we put into place over a year ago to score their 5S for their workplace cleanliness and organization. All joking aside, these were all critical improvements that helped the throughput of work in the shop. Once again, Speed, Quality, Service.

That evening was the Celebration Feast at the best Cajun food restaurant around. It was a humble but charming place inside the local Holiday Inn. That is unassuming enough, but I can attest to the validity of that claim. Best of all, the fabulous food came with a big helping of home-cooked Cajun hospitality.

I was one of the first to arrive, so I grabbed a draft beer and had a seat at the bar. No sooner had I sat down, a tall, handsome, burly young man with a full, dark beard came over to me with a huge smile and stretched out his hand.

"Well, hullo there, you must be Mr. Mark," he said.

I looked up from my beer, somewhat startled, and nodded as I swallowed, setting the glass on the bar. I held out my hand for a shake. "Yes, that's me," I said with a smile.

"Very good, my friend," he said with his thick Cajun accent. "Gerry said you might be arriving before the rest of them. I'm Jean-Paul, Gerry's first cousin. Everybody calls me JP." He said this with a smile and hunch of his broad shoulders. "I'm the manager here."

He was referring to Gerry, the general manager of Versitec. "Oh, yes," I said. Gerry mentioned that his family was in the restaurant business.

JP nodded his head. "Yes, my family owns this restaurant here and two others in Baton Rouge. I guess you could say it's in our blood," he said with a wink.

Just then, I heard my name called out. When I turned to look, Gerry and Mike, the director of operations, had just arrived. They strolled over to where JP and I were chatting. Gerry gave him a big bear hug, "Hey, so good to see you, brother."

"You the same," he replied.

"I hope you've got something special planned for tonight's menu. It's a big occasion, and we have an honored guest with us—a friend all the way from Ohio, Mr. Buckeye here, who's eager to try some real Cajun cooking before he heads back." Gerry said this with a grin, resting a hand on my shoulder, a nod to my Ohio roots and my passion for Ohio State Buckeye football.

JP nodded, and with a big smile underneath his thick black beard, he said, "Oh, don't worry about that. We will be sure to give you a little taste of the bayou before you leave. Now, why don't you gentlemen have a seat, and we'll be right over to get your drinks?"

Slowly, the Versitec side of the restaurant began to fill as several more employees, spouses, partners, kids, and guests arrived, bringing many friendly introductions. It took only a short time for the crowd to exceed JP's reserved area for Versitec. It didn't seem to matter. Even those guests who were not part of our party seemed to know many who were. Before long, it was as if we took over the entire restaurant that evening: a testament to the legacy of Versitec within the community and Gerry's leadership team.

Soon, the food started coming, first the appetizers, then the main course, albeit difficult to determine where the appetizers stopped and the main course started, with a wide variety of seafood, alligator bites (yes, genuine alligator), crawfish, Andouille sausage, softshell crab, seafood gumbo, and chicken and shrimp jambalaya. I took a bite of everything and more, before my main course, the crawfish etouffee, arrived, and it was an excellent choice. Then, of course, a slice of king cake and a scoop of ice cream for dessert.

The dinner lasted at least an hour, with the drinks getting stronger and the stories longer. I sat in awe of the Cajun dialect that transformed even the most mundane topics into a melody of authentic linguistic style. With my stomach full and thirst nearly quenched, I listened to my guests tease each other and embellish the same old stories, making them more interesting each time. It was a beautiful thing.

Finally, Gerry stood up and, with a clang of his spoon against his wine glass, interrupted their stories, asking for their attention.

"Hello, my friends!" he exclaimed, raising his hands in the air. "It's time to stop telling all those lies and behave ourselves." He flashed a big smile, coaxing everyone to join in. "We're about to kick off the real show for the evening—our annual Celebration. It's wonderful to see so many of our team members here tonight, along with all those who are important to you. Welcome, we're thrilled you're here. Even better, we welcome several of our colleagues who have been working with Versitec throughout the past year on various projects and initiatives. We're delighted to have you here."

Gerry sipped his beer and then continued, "Here's to new friends!" He raised his mug and his voice at the same time. "Now, let's get on with our agenda for this evening. As you know, the rules are quite simple. All eight teams will take turns telling us about their biggest success and their biggest setback of the year. Lastly, they will tell us what they learned the most about living out our company values."

The Team Celebration had been held annually for twenty-three years, and the rules were very familiar for most. It was introduced by Hal, the original owner, as a way to celebrate the past year and learn from one another. Gerry paused, looked around the room, and asked, "Are we ready to roll?"

Everyone nodded, and Bobby, the team leader of the Emergency Maintenance Repair Team, stood up and walked over to the podium. He greeted everyone and began with the team's most significant accomplishment of the year: opening the large vessel maintenance bay, which went operational in February. Their most significant setback or failure was failing to meet their TPM (Total Productive Maintenance) goal for the year.

Although it all seemed straightforward, Bobby's stories, provided with saucy details, made everyone laugh out loud one minute and tugged at their heartstrings the next. The theme for the maintenance team was to continue to innovate and improve. In both cases, the success of the large bay repair cell and the fact that they fell short of reaching their goal of 100% TPM were examples of the team constantly striving to be better.

We all gave Bobby and the team a great ovation as they stood and smiled, then raised a glass for a toast—a proud tradition and remnant of Versitec's earliest days.

Once Bobby and the team took a seat and the applause had finished, Gerry stood and thanked him and the team for their fantastic work. Then, without wasting time, he announced that Glenda and the Small Vessel Repair Team were up next. With that, Glenda and Andy jumped up and strode up to the podium.

Not being the least bit shy, Glenda jumped right in, "Good evening, everyone. We're certainly happy to be here tonight to share our team's journey this year with you. I've brought my friend Andy here to help share our story.

"Before we do that, however, I want to take a brief moment to recognize one of our guests here tonight, our friend and teammate Mark." She smiled and waved her hand to tell me to wave to the crowd. "Mr. Mark here has helped us tremendously with our efforts to streamline the work that was coming through our area with all of the Lean process improvements and 5S work we have been doing over the past several months. We're just tickled to have him here to join us and eat some good Cajun food."

I smiled, bigger this time, and waved back at Glenda.

She recounted her story: "The two stories that we have for you tonight are a direct result of all the work we've been doing over the past year. We want to celebrate our first 100% monthly On-Time Delivery score. To explain how we achieved this goal, here's Andy."

Andy smiled as he approached the podium. "Thank you, Glenda," he began. "As mentioned, we achieved our first 100% On-Time Delivery in March. This was no small feat. In my twenty-two years with Versitec, we've rarely, if ever, hit this mark, and we've only tracked it for the past six years." He paused before continuing. "It might seem discouraging, but we've come to understand the importance of this measure. In our complex work environment, with tight turnarounds, 100% On-Time Delivery felt like an impossible goal."

The employees, including Gerry and the leadership team, nodded in agreement. Andy went on. "We all know our work is mostly triage—projects are often overdue the moment they hit the shop. But after attending Mr. Buckeye's training, we shifted our mindset." With a playful nod my way, he added, "We made two key changes: First, we collaborated more closely with the maintenance and facilities teams in the local petrochemical plants, focusing on planning and scheduling. Second, we reevaluated how we handled emergency jobs. By applying 5S and Lean principles, we gained better control and confidence in our turnaround times.

"These efforts led to our first OTD measures last September. Initially, our performance was just over 39%, but we kept improving. Glenda and the planning team worked closely with our customers, and eventually we achieved our first month of 100% On-Time Delivery. Since then, our OTD has averaged just over 97% for the past five months. This was our team's biggest success this past year."

Andy then turned to his teammate with a frown. "Now, Glenda will share our biggest failure for the year."

Andy stepped away from the podium as Glenda returned. Glenda stepped up to the podium in her usual bold, confident manner. Addressing the crowd, she said, "Thank you, Andy, for sharing that story with us. The changes and improvements that the team has made in the shop are quite amazing, and I might add, I should know, I've been here for twenty-three years, and the small vessel work area has never looked better." She gave a big thumbs-up to Andy and the team.

Then she went on. "Well, as you know, not everything goes as planned, and that is what we specialize in at Versitec: our ability to handle maintenance emergencies for our customers. When a piece of safety equipment fails at one of the processing plants, the entire plant is down for all practical purposes, equating to thousands of dollars an hour in processing time.

"On Thanksgiving Eve, two of our biggest customers had their quarterly preventive maintenance planned for the long weekend. Twelve of our employees agreed to work on the holiday shift in exchange for a longer break once the job was completed. We did not expect any issues.

"However, during the inspections, we found that several valves were showing signs of distress. We chose to repair and reset them, which meant taking them back to the shop along with four technicians. The rest of the crew stayed on-site, performing regular maintenance checks and minor repairs.

"Everything was going smoothly until the second shift arrived. Shortly after the shift change, we received an emergency call from one of our other customers, who needed an urgent response at their site almost sixty miles away.

"We held a quick meeting on-site. Nate, Richey, and Samantha hesitated to accept the request but ultimately agreed. It was one of our biggest clients, and we had no option but to recall our first-shift employees to cover the job. This began our Thanksgiving weekend, filled with twelve-hour shifts. Our hardworking employees sacrificed their time off to get the job done.

"Despite being tempted to ask Gerry's advice, we decided not to disturb him on Thanksgiving Day. After discussing it with the team, I made the 'executive' decision to accept the emergency request. Our first shift team completed the shop work, while the second shift took the emergency call."

Glenda stopped speaking for a moment and took a sip of her drink. Then, in a calm and reflective manner, she said, "We did complete the job, but we had a significant failure during the process." She explained how Jonna, one of their team members, had been involved in an accident while using the crane to move a large valve. The incident occurred during the second shift on the Friday following Thanksgiving. While working on locating the valve on a test fixture, Jonna's hand got caught between the hoisting belt and the valve itself and was dragged for about ten feet before her colleagues could stop the motion and come to her aid. In her retelling, it was clear Glenda remained upset by the incident, and she looked at Jonna with a tear in her eye. She mouthed an apology to Jonna, who sat there with a bandage still wrapped around her wrist. Jonna waved with her injured hand and gave a big smile.

"This accident was bad enough, but it could have been much worse. As most of you know, we go to great lengths to ensure we all remain safe in this crazy (and dangerous) workplace. We have always taken pride in doing things in the safest way possible. However, something must be said for being just plain tired and exhausted, and we know better. That is when accidents happen. That is a failure."

Glenda smiled now as she said, "Let's all show Jonna how much we love her. We are all hoping and praying for a quick recovery. And when you do get back, we have a job waiting for you in the office, behind a desk. At least for as long as you want it."

Jonna shouted, "I'll take it!"

Everyone burst out laughing, and the mood in the room lightened.

Then Gerry stood up and said, "OK, Glenda and Andy, which of you will tell us about your biggest lessons learned?"

Glenda motioned for Andy to come up again.

When he got to the podium, he didn't hesitate. "Leadership! It was leadership that I think we learned most of all. At least the way we understand leadership around here. Everyone has leadership potential and the capacity to lead in any situation where their leadership might be needed. With Hal before and now with Gerry, we always say 'lead from where you are at any given moment.' That's what our team has done. We are a team of leaders, without a doubt. This way, when we win, and win a lot, we win as a team of respected leaders. We do not relinquish accountability and integrity when we fail to meet our high expectations."

Andy took a deep breath before continuing. "I understand that what I'm about to say may sound like high-brow stuff for someone who has worked as a technician for the past twenty-three years, but it's the honest truth: It only works when we have someone like Gerry leading us." He pointed to Gerry, who tried to deflect the attention but eventually waved at the crowd. Emotions ran high in this part of the world and were shared by all.

Then Glenda said, "After Jonna's accident, I took it pretty hard. I felt responsible for going forward with all that work simultaneously, which led to the accident. But from the moment Gerry became aware of what happened, he was there to support me, Jonna, and our entire team throughout the entire period."

As Andy and Glenda shared their heartfelt reflections, the room was filled with a profound sense of unity and respect. Their words reminded everyone that true leadership isn't about titles or positions; it's about stepping up, supporting one another, and holding ourselves accountable, especially during challenging times. This "celebration" wasn't just about hitting targets or achieving milestones; it was about recognizing the strength and resilience of a team that leads from every corner and lifts each other up in moments of triumph and adversity alike. Together, they had learned that the greatest victories come not just from meeting expectations, but from the shared journey of growth, leadership, and unwavering support for one another.

PART THREE
SUMMIT

CHAPTER TWELVE

Answering the Call to Elevated Leadership

There you have it. Now you know the inspirations and stories about how E3C3: The Six Core Elements of Elevated Leadership was revealed to me and how a few of the Elevated Leaders I have known and admired proved them true. My hat goes off to all of them. They show us what it means to lead others to higher levels of success.

These stories about Elevated Leaders will help others understand and appreciate the power and simplicity of the Six Core Elements. Most of all, they will provide examples of what they might look like when put into practice.

I know many more leaders like these have their own stories to tell. I have a sense that you know a few Elevated Leaders as well. In fact, anyone reading these words is or could be an Elevated Leader simply by answering the call to lead, focusing on these Six Core Elements, and seeking ways to incorporate them into their lives and relationships at work and outside of work.

This is a good thing because the need for Elevated Leadership has never been more acute, whether in the workplace or our society as a whole. As people continue to turn ever-inward toward themselves, aided by dependencies on technology, the need for the human touch has never been so great. This void will only grow at an ever-alarming rate unless we rise above it to fill the void. With the recent advent of artificial intelligence, the very meaning of what it means to be human will be questioned. However,

I believe there is something simple and quite divine that we can do to fill many of these voids, and that is to adopt an Elevated Leadership mindset and heartset, then start to focus on how we can elevate ourselves and others by incorporating E3C3: The Six Core Elements of Elevated Leadership into our daily lives.

Everyone has the potential to embody Elevated Leadership, as it includes everyone. When we sacrifice to uplift those around us for greater success, we embody the essence of Elevated Leadership. Some may find this assertion bold or even absurd. What about people's limitations, backgrounds, or faults? To that, I ask: What about their possibilities, their life's purpose, their unique cultural heritage, and inherent beauty? Elevated Leadership transcends boundaries and appears in diverse forms. It may vary in appearance based on our perspectives and experiences. Still, the fundamental question remains: Is this individual someone I would willingly follow for collective progress toward a shared goal? Let's explore what this looks like at every level of leadership.

Answering the Call to Lead Ourselves

We are all called to be Elevated Leaders, and that journey begins with leading ourselves. Self-leadership is often seen as the highest form of leadership because without it, we cannot hope to lead others. But what does this mean? It's simple, though not always easy: it starts with adopting the mindset and heartset necessary to position ourselves for success.

When faced with situations that demand self-leadership, we encounter the call to Elevated Leadership. In that moment, we have a choice: to lean in, meet the challenge, and lead, or to step back, defer, and avoid it. This choice isn't about your role, title, or last promotion—it's about a personal commitment to sacrifice a little (or sometimes more than a little) of yourself to help others succeed.

To elevate our personal growth, we must start with self-awareness and an openness to feedback, insights, and guidance from others. Leadership is a continuous journey; your development as a leader never truly ends, as there are always new opportunities to grow. Failing to embrace this journey means risking your full potential, often due to the lack of honesty, vulnerability, and authenticity that self-leadership demands.

To be an Elevated Leader, it's crucial to cultivate both the mindset and heartset needed to face challenges head-on, even when the path is unclear. These moments of uncertainty are where your most profound learning occurs. Embrace the willingness to make behavioral changes—that is what is essential to become a more effective self-leader. The Six Core Elements serve as a guiding framework for this ongoing journey.

The Six Core Elements of Leading Yourself

Leading yourself with the Six Core Elements of Elevated Leadership as your foundation means fully committing to your growth and development. The following explains how these Six Core Elements and their supporting competencies help shape effective self-leadership.

Embrace: Leading yourself begins with embracing your strengths, weaknesses, and areas for growth. You cultivate self-awareness and authenticity by accepting yourself fully and acknowledging your abilities and limitations.
Supporting Competencies:

- **Self-Awareness:** Understanding your emotions, strengths, weaknesses, and how they impact others.
- **Authenticity:** Being genuine and true to your values and beliefs in your actions.
- **Emotional Intelligence:** Managing your emotions and understanding how they affect your behavior.
- **Integrity:** Acting consistently with your values, maintaining honesty, and ethical behavior.
- **Personal Accountability:** Taking responsibility for your actions, decisions, and outcomes.

Empower: Empowering yourself involves setting goals, making decisions, and acting to achieve them. You build confidence and self-efficacy by taking initiative and holding yourself accountable for your actions and outcomes.
Supporting Competencies:

- **Self-Efficacy:** Believing in your ability to achieve goals and make decisions.
- **Goal Orientation:** Setting and striving to achieve meaningful goals.
- **Initiative:** Taking proactive steps to accomplish tasks and solve problems.
- **Decision-Making:** Making informed and timely decisions that align with your values and goals.
- **Resilience:** Bouncing back from setbacks and staying focused on your objectives.

Engage: Engaging yourself means staying focused, motivated, and committed to your goals. You harness your inner drive and determination by maintaining a positive mindset, staying disciplined, and persevering through challenges.

Supporting Competencies:

- **Motivation:** Harnessing your inner drive to stay committed to your goals.
- **Discipline:** Maintaining consistent effort and focusing on your objectives.
- **Focus:** Staying attentive and avoiding distractions to achieve your goals.
- **Perseverance:** Continuing to strive toward goals despite obstacles or difficulties.
- **Positive Attitude:** Maintaining an optimistic outlook even in challenging situations.

Challenge: Challenging yourself entails stepping out of your comfort zone, taking risks, and embracing new growth opportunities. You foster resilience and adaptability by pushing yourself beyond your limits and embracing change.

Supporting Competencies:

- **Adaptability:** Being flexible and open to new experiences and changes.

- **Risk-Taking:** Being willing to step out of your comfort zone and embrace uncertainty.
- **Learning Agility:** Continuously seeking new knowledge and learning from experiences.
- **Innovation:** Embracing creativity and new ideas to solve problems.
- **Resilience:** Strengthening your ability to recover from challenges and bounce back stronger.

Coach: Coaching yourself involves seeking feedback, reflecting on your experiences, and continuously learning and improving. By soliciting input from others, evaluating your performance, and pursuing opportunities for self-improvement, you cultivate a growth mindset and strive for excellence.

Supporting Competencies:

- **Self-Reflection**: Regularly evaluating your performance and experiences to learn and improve.
- **Feedback Seeking**: Actively seeking input from others to enhance your growth.
- **Growth Mindset**: Believing that your abilities can be developed through effort and learning.
- **Continuous Learning**: Pursuing opportunities to develop new skills and knowledge.
- **Performance Improvement**: Focusing on enhancing your effectiveness and achieving excellence.

Celebrate: Celebrating yourself means recognizing and acknowledging your achievements, milestones, and progress. By celebrating your successes, big and small, and expressing gratitude for your efforts and accomplishments, you nurture a sense of self-worth and fulfillment.

Supporting Competencies:

- **Self-Recognition**: Acknowledging your achievements and progress.
- **Gratitude**: Expressing appreciation for your efforts and successes.
- **Positive Reinforcement**: Encouraging yourself by celebrating small wins.

- **Self-Worth**: Valuing your accomplishments and feeling confident in your abilities.
- **Mindfulness**: Being present and appreciating the journey, not just the outcomes.

Answering the Call When Leading Others

Every thriving team boasts a capable leader—someone others willingly follow, recognizing in them the core elements of Elevated Leadership: Embrace, Empower, Engage, Challenge, Coach, and Celebrate. This truth resonates deeply with me, and I admire the remarkable team leaders I have encountered throughout my career. They will always hold a special place in my heart. Why? One of the most challenging transitions for a leader is moving from self-leadership to leading others. It's a pivotal moment where leaders learn invaluable lessons. Firstly, it's no longer solely about oneself. Secondly, it entails sacrificing a piece of oneself for the collective good of the team. Lastly, leadership is inherently messy and far from easy. However, the returns on investing time and effort into becoming an Elevated Leader are potentially immense.

Moreover, it is crucial to acknowledge that while formal team leaders exist in every team, the dynamic nature of modern work often necessitates the emergence of leadership, even if only temporarily, to fill any leadership voids that might open up during the course of your team's work. Exceptional team leadership is a collaborative effort spearheaded by Elevated Leaders. As Simon Sinek points out, "Leadership is a team sport."

If the call to lead remains unanswered at the team level, the team will never realize its full potential and stay trapped in these leadership voids. Eventually, this void leads to disengagement, dwindling interest, and a lack of heartfelt motivation. The next time you encounter a leadership gap within your team, consider what actions you, as an Elevated Leader, can take to fill that void, regardless of your position within the team.

The Six Core Elements of Leading Others

Leading others with the Six Core Elements of Elevated Leadership as the foundation entails guiding and inspiring individuals to achieve shared goals and objectives. The highest performing teams are teams of leaders, individuals who are prepared and equipped to step up, lean in and accept accountability, whenever the situation calls for it. Here's how each of the Six Core Elements and supporting key competencies can help to increase effectiveness when leading others from a team perspective.

Embrace: Leading others begins with embracing their unique strengths, perspectives, and contributions. By recognizing and valuing the diversity within the team, leaders create an inclusive environment where everyone feels respected and empowered to contribute their best.
Supporting Competencies:

- **Inclusion:** Creating an environment where diverse perspectives are valued and everyone feels included.
- **Empathy:** Understanding and appreciating the feelings and perspectives of others.
- **Cultural Competence:** Recognizing and respecting cultural differences within the team.
- **Emotional Intelligence:** Managing relationships effectively by understanding and responding to others' emotions.
- **Relationship Building:** Developing strong, trust-based relationships with team members.

Empower: Empowering others involves delegating authority, providing autonomy, and fostering a sense of ownership and accountability. By entrusting individuals with responsibilities and giving them the freedom to make decisions, leaders empower them to take initiative and drive results.
Supporting Competencies:

- **Delegation:** Assigning responsibility and authority to others to encourage ownership and accountability.
- **Trust-Building**: Establishing and maintaining trust within the team by empowering individuals.
- **Autonomy:** Encouraging individuals to take initiative and make decisions independently.

- **Motivating Others:** Inspiring team members to take action and achieve their goals.
- **Accountability:** Holding team members responsible for their performance and outcomes.

Engage: Engaging others means fostering open communication, listening actively, and soliciting feedback. By creating opportunities for dialogue and collaboration, leaders ensure that everyone feels heard, valued, and invested in the team's success.

Supporting Competencies:

- **Active Listening:** Fully concentrating, understanding, and responding to team members' concerns and ideas.
- **Communication:** Clearly conveying information and ensuring understanding within the team.
- **Collaboration:** Fostering teamwork and cooperative efforts among team members.
- **Feedback Seeking:** Encouraging team members to share their thoughts and feedback.
- **Conflict Management:** Addressing and resolving conflicts in a constructive manner to maintain engagement.

Challenge: Challenging others involves setting high expectations, pushing individuals to stretch beyond their comfort zones, and encouraging continuous growth and development. Leaders inspire excellence and innovation by providing opportunities for learning and development and pushing individuals to reach their full potential.

Supporting Competencies:

- **Goal Setting:** Establishing clear, challenging goals that motivate and stretch team members.
- **Performance Management:** Monitoring and managing the performance of team members to ensure continuous improvement.
- **Innovation:** Encouraging creative thinking and the development of new ideas within the team.

- **Resilience Building:** Helping team members develop the ability to recover from setbacks and challenges.
- **Talent Development:** Identifying and nurturing the potential within team members to help them grow.

Coach: Coaching others entails providing guidance, support, and mentorship to help individuals overcome challenges and maximize their potential. By offering constructive feedback, sharing insights, and providing mentorship, leaders empower individuals to grow and develop their skills.

Supporting Competencies:

- **Mentoring:** Providing guidance and sharing expertise to help others develop.
- **Constructive Feedback:** Offering feedback that is specific, actionable, and aimed at improving performance.
- **Developmental Conversations:** Engaging in discussions focused on personal and professional growth.
- **Supportiveness:** Being approachable and available to assist team members with their challenges.
- **Empathy:** Understanding and addressing the unique developmental needs of each team member.

Celebrate: Celebrating others involves recognizing and acknowledging their accomplishments, milestones, and contributions. Leaders foster a culture of positivity, motivation, and camaraderie within the team by publicly acknowledging achievements and expressing appreciation for their efforts.

Supporting Competencies:

- **Recognition:** Acknowledging the achievements and contributions of team members.
- **Positive Reinforcement:** Encouraging desired behaviors by celebrating successes.
- **Appreciation:** Expressing gratitude for the efforts and contributions of others.

- **Team Spirit:** Fostering a sense of camaraderie and collective pride within the team.
- **Motivation:** Using celebration as a tool to keep team members motivated and engaged.

Answering the Call When Leading Other Leaders

Leading other leaders is a distinct and challenging responsibility. It involves guiding and inspiring individuals who already possess strong leadership qualities, while fostering an environment where they can thrive, contribute their unique perspectives, and collaborate effectively toward shared goals. In this role, you are not just leading; you are modeling Elevated Leadership for every leader in the organization to follow.

This level of leadership requires a deep commitment to the principles of Elevated Leadership. It's about more than just managing; it's about cultivating a culture of excellence, where every leader is empowered to elevate their team and, by extension, the organization as a whole. The transition from leading a team to leading other leaders is profound—one that demands a higher level of self-awareness, strategic vision, and the ability to inspire others to rise to the occasion.

As an Elevated Leader, your influence extends beyond your immediate team. You set the tone for leadership across the organization, ensuring that the values of Embrace, Empower, Engage, Challenge, Coach, and Celebrate are not just understood but are lived out daily by all leaders. The impact of your leadership is amplified as you guide others to lead with the same principles, creating a ripple effect of positive change.

If the call to lead other leaders is not answered, the organization risks stagnation, missed opportunities, and failure to reach its full potential. In contrast, when you embrace this call, you not only enhance the effectiveness of other leaders but also contribute to the overall strength and resilience of the organization.

The Six Core Elements of Leading Other Leaders

The Six Core Elements of Elevated Leadership is a framework for leading other leaders effectively. The elements serve as a foundation for inspiring, guiding, and developing leadership at every level of the organization. The following sections will delve into how each of these elements, along with their supporting key competencies, can enhance your effectiveness in leading other leaders from an organizational perspective.

Embrace: Leading other leaders begins with embracing their strengths, talents, and diverse viewpoints. Recognizing and appreciating their contributions fosters a culture of mutual respect and collaboration.
Supporting Competencies:

- **Inclusive Leadership:** Creating an environment where diverse perspectives among leaders are valued and encouraged.
- **Visionary Thinking:** Recognizing and leveraging the unique talents and perspectives of other leaders to shape a shared vision.
- **Strategic Relationship Building:** Building and maintaining strong relationships with other leaders to foster collaboration and mutual respect.
- **Emotional Intelligence:** Understanding and managing the emotions and motivations of other leaders to enhance team dynamics.
- **Cultural Competence:** Appreciating and leveraging cultural diversity within the leadership team to drive innovation and collaboration.

Empower: Empowering other leaders involves delegating authority, providing autonomy, and entrusting them with significant responsibilities. Empowering them to make decisions and take ownership of their initiatives fosters a sense of ownership and accountability.
Supporting Competencies:

- **Delegation:** Effectively distributing responsibilities among other leaders to promote autonomy and ownership.
- **Empowerment:** Encouraging other leaders to take initiative and make decisions within their areas of responsibility.
- **Trust-Building:** Cultivating a high-trust environment where other leaders feel confident in taking bold actions.

- **Accountability:** Ensuring that other leaders are responsible for their actions and the outcomes of their decisions.
- **Motivating Others:** Inspiring other leaders to perform at their best by providing the autonomy and resources they need.

Engage: Engaging other leaders entails fostering open communication channels, encouraging dialogue, and actively listening to their ideas and concerns. Involving them in decision-making processes and seeking their input creates a sense of inclusivity and shared purpose.

Supporting Competencies:

- **Communication:** Facilitating open and transparent communication channels with other leaders to encourage dialogue and collaboration.
- **Active Listening:** Giving full attention to the ideas and concerns of other leaders, demonstrating respect and valuing their input.
- **Collaboration:** Promoting a culture of teamwork among leaders, ensuring their efforts are aligned with organizational goals.
- **Feedback Seeking:** Actively seeking input from other leaders to inform decisions and strategies.
- **Conflict Resolution:** Addressing and resolving conflicts among leaders to maintain a cohesive and productive team environment.

Challenge: Challenging other leaders involves setting high expectations, pushing them beyond their comfort zones, and encouraging continuous growth and development. By providing constructive feedback and setting ambitious goals, you inspire them to reach new heights of achievement.

Supporting Competencies:

- **Talent Development:** Identifying growth opportunities for other leaders and challenging them to expand their capabilities.
- **Strategic Thinking:** Encouraging leaders to think critically about long-term goals and strategies, pushing them to innovate.
- **Change Leadership:** Guiding other leaders through change, encouraging them to embrace new challenges and opportunities.

- **Performance Management:** Setting high standards for other leaders and providing the support needed to achieve them.
- **Innovation:** Challenging leaders to think creatively and explore new approaches to solving problems.

Coach: Coaching other leaders entails providing guidance, mentorship, and support to help them overcome challenges and maximize their potential. By offering feedback, sharing insights, and providing opportunities for skill development, you facilitate their professional growth and success.

Supporting Competencies:

- **Strategic Mentorship:** Guiding other leaders in developing strategic thinking and navigating complex challenges.
- **Targeted Feedback:** Offering specific, actionable feedback tailored to enhance decision-making and influence.
- **Executive Development:** Engaging in discussions focused on long-term growth, succession planning, and leadership style.
- **Strategic Support:** Acting as a partner and advisor, providing the tools and insights needed to lead teams effectively.
- **Empathetic Understanding:** Addressing the unique pressures faced by other leaders, offering support for resilience and adaptability.

Celebrate: Celebrating other leaders involves recognizing and appreciating their accomplishments, milestones, and contributions. Acknowledging their achievements and publicly praising their efforts reinforces a culture of positivity, motivation, and camaraderie.

Supporting Competencies:

- **Recognition:** Acknowledging the achievements and contributions of other leaders to reinforce positive behaviors and outcomes.
- **Appreciation:** Expressing gratitude for the efforts of other leaders, fostering a positive and motivating environment.
- **Public Acknowledgment**: Celebrating the successes of other leaders in visible ways to inspire others and build morale.

- **Team Spirit:** Promoting a culture of camaraderie and mutual support among leaders.
- **Positive Reinforcement:** Using celebration as a tool to reinforce the behaviors and attitudes that contribute to success.

Summary: Answering the Call to Elevated Leadership

Answering the call to Elevated Leadership requires embracing the interconnected roles of Leading Yourself, Leading Others, and Leading Other Leaders. Each perspective is crucial on its own, but the true power of leadership emerges when these three elements are integrated.

Leading Yourself is the foundation, as self-leadership builds the discipline, self-awareness, and authenticity necessary for personal and professional growth. Leading Others extends this influence by guiding and inspiring teams, fostering collaboration, and driving collective success. Finally, Leading Other Leaders amplifies your impact across the organization, shaping a culture of excellence and empowering other leaders to elevate their teams.

When these three perspectives come together, they create a cohesive and dynamic approach to leadership that drives not only individual and team success but also the overall strength and resilience of the organization. Elevated Leadership is about cultivating a holistic leadership journey—one that begins with the self, extends to the team, and ultimately influences the entire organization.

Final Descent

KM and the rest of our motley crew finally reunited with what remained of the summit team a few hours later at Camp Muir. The relief of being back together was palpable, and we were eager to hear their account of the journey. They all expressed genuine concern for the challenges we faced and wished us well. I couldn't help but notice Jonathan, the software engineer from Seattle, visibly struggling from sheer exhaustion. As I observed his state, I couldn't help but wonder what condition I would have been in if I had attempted to summit.

After a well-deserved hour of rest, we packed up and began our descent down the mountain, traversing the snowfield and eventually reaching the upper levels of the maintained trails that would lead us back to Paradise Inn and the conclusion of our adventure. As I approached the end, Gregg, our lead guide, stepped in to walk alongside me for the last few hundred yards.

"Mark, how are you feeling about this whole experience? I know that decision up there wasn't an easy one, but I think you'll agree it was the right one."

I nodded and smiled broadly. "Honestly, I'm thrilled with the entire experience. Before, I could only imagine what it would be like; now I know that reality far surpassed any of my expectations. And most importantly, everyone is returning safely."

Gregg glanced at me, my reflection visible in his mirrored goggles, and smiled. "That's right," he said.

Other than on our wedding day, I've never been happier to see my wife than when I arrived back at the hotel, utterly exhausted and in desperate need of a hot shower and a good meal. A pang of guilt washed over me as I saw her face, knowing how worried she must have been. But after all the hugs and kisses, she asked, "Are you happy now?"

I nodded, "Yes, I can't even begin to describe the experience, but it was incredible."

She smiled, but her expression revealed her conflicting emotions—angry at me for putting her through this ordeal, yet happy that I had finally achieved my goal. One thing I know for sure: she couldn't care less whether I reached the summit or not.

"Good, I'm happy too. Happy you're here," she said, giving me another big hug. Then, waving her hand and turning up her nose, she added, "Now, go take a hot shower—you need it."

Reflecting on my Mt. Rainier adventure, it's clear that I was climbing more than just a mountain—I was navigating the heights and challenges of life itself. Even now, as I write these words, I'm still climbing, still pursuing dreams and goals, creating learning opportunities from new experiences, and growing as a result. Yet, I've also come to realize that this journey isn't one I can make alone. It requires a deep belief in something greater and the support of other leaders—which is where you come in.

The inspiration I drew from that experience cemented my commitment to write and publish this book, but my mission extends far beyond that. I'm driven to share the E3C3 framework and the Six Core Elements with as many people as possible and to enlist their help in spreading this approach.

So, I ask you: What is your summit? What goals are you, your team, or your organization striving to achieve? Why are these goals important? How do you plan to reach them? And perhaps most crucially, how do you want to feel about the journey, the people you work with, and your organization when you reach your summit?

This is where the implementation of E3C3 Leadership begins—right here, with these questions, as we embark on the path together.

CHAPTER THIRTEEN

Implementing Elevated Leadership

"Sometime today, tomorrow, or later this week, you will likely experience a leadership void. Whether personally, within your team, within your bigger organization, or a combination of all three, you will come upon a leadership void." — Jim, the GM

When it comes to encountering a leadership void, it's not a matter of "if" but "when." You and I will likely face several leadership voids of varying magnitudes over the next few weeks. When you start to sense that uneasy feeling that the need for leadership is going unmet, you will have to ask yourself, "What am I going to do about this?"

This may surprise some. You might not see yourself as a leader, but that would be a mistake. Similarly, we might not view others as leaders, which is also a mistake. Leadership is for everyone. Each of us has the potential to be a leader. In fact, your organization needs everyone to step up and lead in their own way when necessary to fill the leadership voids that constantly arise. The good news is that this is the most straightforward part: it's simply a matter of choice and embracing a shared leadership mindset and heartset.

When faced with leadership voids, it's common to look to our top leaders—like the Senior Vice-Presidents or CEO—for action. While it's fair to hold them accountable, it's crucial to recognize that no single leader, no matter how capable, can fill all the voids across the organization. Addressing these gaps effectively requires a collective team of accountable leaders.

This doesn't mean that the executive staff doesn't play a critical role in raising leadership capacity. They are ultimately responsible for all leadership voids, but they cannot do it alone. Executives can and should set the tone by clearly stating the organization's leadership expectations. They must demonstrate their commitment through engagement and inclusion by holding themselves and everyone in the organization accountable for meeting these expectations.

A leadership team united in its commitment to increasing leadership capacity is the first and most critical step in creating an elevated organization. But this is just the beginning. With the executives leading the way to the summit, the arduous task of bringing everyone else along for the journey begins. This is where leadership development comes in. It is the key to achieving elevation and will continue to distinguish the best organizations from the rest. To succeed, you must tap into and develop the leadership capacity of every contributor.

Just as a mountain guide leads climbers up a mountain, every team member must be connected to the same rope, committed to learning and developing the skills and behaviors necessary to reach the summit and ensure the entire team's safety. Regardless of the size of the leadership gaps, every team member is expected to step up, take responsibility, accept accountability, and do what it takes to reach the summit together and return safely. This approach, which I call Elevated Leadership, requires that every team member at all levels of the organization believes in and commits to developing their leadership potential through continuous learning and development.

Building the Foundation for Elevated Leadership

Throughout my career in leadership development, I've had the privilege of working with and learning from exceptional Elevated Leaders across various organizations, from individual contributors to CEOs. Regardless of role or position, I've witnessed firsthand how some leaders successfully drove critical business transformations by leading their teams and organizations through leadership development initiatives.

The organizations that achieved the most success—those that elevated their leadership capabilities—invested time, money, and effort into building a strong, culturally sound foundation upon which to scale their leadership development efforts and deliver real impact. Conversely, those that were less successful often failed to establish this foundation.

While recognizing that every organization is unique and that leadership development must be tailored to fit specific contexts, I've identified six key building blocks that every organization—regardless of how different they may be—must establish to lay the groundwork for Elevated Leadership development:

1. Adopt an Elevated Leadership Mindset
2. Balance the Scales of Performance
3. Foster Leadership Accountability
4. Identify Leadership Voids
5. Implement The Six Core Elements of Elevated Leadership
6. Take Action

These building blocks form the bedrock of an Elevated Leadership development initiative, ensuring that organizations not only survive but thrive in their transformational journeys.

Adopt an Elevated Leadership Mindset:

Elevated Leadership hinges on a collective commitment to developing leadership potential in every individual. Before the ascent to the summit, every climber hooks onto the rope. At that moment, you are not just a team member—you are also a leader. Your actions, or lack thereof, will directly and significantly impact your fellow climbers, who are also connected to the rope. You and everyone on your team must adopt an Elevated Leadership mindset and heartset. It becomes clear that your success in reaching the summit and returning safely depends entirely on the success of everyone else on your team doing the same. The work you engage in daily with your team and others within your organization is no different. I'm sure you have some lofty goals, so remember, Sir Edmund Hillary did not make it to the summit of Everest by himself.

Similarly, the organizations that will continue to prosper in the future are those that recognize leadership is not reserved for a select group of people. Leadership development should include everyone, regardless of their role or position. This is the essence of Elevated Leadership. Every team member must adopt and embrace a leadership mindset and heartset. It comes down to answering the following two questions affirmatively:

Question #1: Am I willing to be an Elevated Leader, committed to leading myself and others to higher levels of success?

Question #2: Am I willing to do what it takes to develop and increase my own and others' leadership capacity?

These are questions that everyone in the organization must ask themselves and answer affirmatively to achieve elevation. At first, you may not feel like a leader or see yourself as one, but if you believe you are an Elevated Leader, you soon will be. Or perhaps you already see yourself as a leader, which is fantastic. I challenge you to periodically reflect on these questions and reaffirm your commitment with renewed conviction. We need everyone to be "all in."

Elevated Leadership lies not in a specific role, position, or title, but in a culture that everyone within the organization can nurture and foster. Whether you're the CEO, VP, director, manager, team leader, or trusted colleague, true leadership capability is only possible with a commitment to leadership development. It starts with developing oneself and then progresses to developing others.

With this shared organizational commitment to Elevated Leadership, you and your team must define what that means in your own terms, aligned with your strategic objectives. In simpler terms, ask: "What are the goals for me and my team? How would we describe success?"

From here, the fundamental question that must be answered is this: "Do we have the leadership capacity to achieve our goals?" Perhaps more importantly, we should ask: "What and where are the leadership voids that might prevent our team from reaching its goals?" Intuitively, we can only identify these voids if we have clearly defined and described our leadership expectations of one another. These expectations will be unique to every individual, team, and organization. However, they will be a combination of knowledge, skills, and behaviors (competencies) aligned with your values and described in terms everyone can understand and relate to.

The ways and means of arriving at your shared leadership expectations can be many and varied. However, we should always view them through the lens of E3C3 and the Six Core Elements of Elevated Leadership, as they provide a simple and practical means of ensuring that your expectations are clear, easy to understand, and assimilate, thereby having the impact they are meant to have.

Balance the Scales of Performance

I once met a leader who said, "When it comes to performance, I don't believe for a minute that anyone in this organization comes to work each morning wanting to do an average job or fall below expectations, whether their own or their manager's."

These are wise words that every leader might agree with. For argument's sake, let's agree to assume that almost everyone wants to know how they and their team are performing and whether their efforts are making a positive impact.

When leading yourself, your team, or your organization to success, the question should be, "What does success look like? How will we know when we are successful, and what are the rules of engagement?"

Peter Drucker, one of the world's most influential management consultants, is credited with the familiar phrase "What gets measured, gets managed." In other words, if something is important enough to manage, it is important enough to measure. The inverse also holds: if it is not essential, then it won't be measured. The question is, what is important to the organization?

When you ask that question, the standard and immediate responses you will get usually point to the obvious—the financials, as they should. The week, the month, and the year, business success will always come down to net income, sales and revenues, managing expenses and other costs.

These are examples of measures that all business ventures track, from small businesses around the corner to the world's largest. However, these are lagging indicators of past performance. More importantly, we should be measuring the things that produce these outcomes, commonly referred to as leading indicators. These are many and varied, but they basically come down to two types of measures: operational and human, or more simply, process and people. These lie on either side of what I call the Balance Scales of Performance.

Process Measures

Process (operational) measures refer to the processes, tools, technologies, machines, methods, data, practices, programs, and so on.: those critical components that define the work we do and how we do it. In the world of business operations, it's all about "hard" data. That's because most of us gravitate toward things that are visibly evident, logical, systematic, tangible, and clearly understood. They are black and white; therefore, we apply more weight and command more attention. A few common examples of Process Measures include:

- Cycle Time
- System Uptime
- Throughput
- Utilization Rate
- On-Time Delivery Rate

People (Human) Measures

However, it takes people to get things done—executing these processes, using these tools, and applying the technologies. For that reason, we must also interact effectively on a human level. Yet, we typically place less weight or importance on the people side of the balance scale. Why is that? Because people come with ideas, attitudes, biases, egos, emotions, dreams, strengths, faults, and life challenges. They are sometimes inconsistent and unpredictable. There are a lot of gray areas when it comes to leading people. It's a messy business, but here are some commonly used People Measures that can help provide a clearer picture:

- Employee Engagement
- Leadership Effectiveness
- Learning and Development Participation
- Employee Productivity
- Employee Well-being

Managing the hard numbers and analyzing the data is easy. Compare that to building relationships, leading and gaining positive influence with people, managing conflict, and developing others. If we're honest, most of us would rather not deal with the people side of performance and shy away from this type of ambiguity and uncertainty. Perhaps this is why employee engagement remains so low, year upon year.

But not Elevated Leaders. They fully understand the importance of learning to influence others in a positive way as the key to achieving superior and lasting results. The bottom line is that your people will always impact performance—how well they feel and what they believe about themselves, their team, and the organization. Is that impact positive or negative? Could it be better? How do your people feel about being a part of your organization? How do they think about those they work with? How do those you lead feel about your leadership? Are your people truly engaged? Elevated Leaders want to know these things.

When you visit the doctor for your annual checkup, you are just as likely to get questions about your mental health and well-being as you are to have your blood pressure checked and your blood tested. Why? Because our health is more than just looking at hard physical data like your cholesterol count. It is equally important to understand how we are doing mentally and emotionally. The doctor gathers this data to make the best diagnosis possible.

Why should our people, teams, or organization be any different? Business organizations are human endeavors as much as operational ones. It involves people executing processes intended to produce a tangible benefit for everyone involved: customers, coworkers, partners, shareholders, etc.

We could discuss all the various metrics organizations have at their disposal regarding organizational performance, especially in the age of big data, but it's unnecessary. The approaches, tools, and methods that any given team or organization will put into practice are many, varied, and unique to each. However, it is paramount that you first seek balance in terms of the amount of weight, attention, and importance placed on both sides of the scale.

For this reason, your first objective in creating what I call the Performance Dynamic is to ensure that regardless of what you are measuring, you and your leaders place an equal emphasis on both operational and human measures.

So, what does excellence or greatness look like for your team? How are you going to measure success? Remember, whatever is essential gets measured, and what gets measured gets done. What are the shared expectations and the few critical Key Performance Indicators most important for you personally and for your team? Have you balanced the scales of performance between both operational and human expectations? Are you clearly stating that you expect everyone in your team to maintain that balance? Only then will you be prepared to bring these two components together, where people are executing processes at the highest level of effectiveness and feel good about the experience. Striking this balance creates what I refer to as the performance dynamic, and it is precisely what is needed for everyone to balance expectations and know the score.

Foster Leadership Accountability

I like to define leadership accountability as holding ourselves and others responsible for the promises we make. Leadership accountability is a good thing, however, when it is lacking it is perhaps the most significant leadership void you will ever encounter. It is typically due to a lack of balance between those operational and human aspects of performance. Too often, we become overly focused on the hard numbers, stealing time and attention away from our people. The reality is, you manage processes, but you lead people.

Consider the classic example of one of your star salespeople, Lucille. Since joining the organization just over two years ago, Lucille has consistently been one of if not the highest-performing salesperson in your company. As her manager, you're impressed by her ability to meet or exceed her sales targets month after month. Her personal management skills are equally impressive, so much so that you promoted her to business development manager.

However, since her promotion, it has become clear that in her hard-driving pursuit of personal results, she has failed to build trusting relationships with her team and has only a passing regard for other management team members. You've received consistent feedback that she micromanages her team, especially when it comes to hitting their sales numbers, while failing to provide the support and direction often needed. This behavior is causing confusion and dysfunction within your team, and other sales staff members are feeling the impact. Most troubling of all, her team is now falling short of its sales goals, and the quality of partner relationships has also been negatively affected.

It's apparent that while Lucille's individual performance has been stellar, in her new role as manager, she's overplaying her operational strength to compensate for her lack of human-focused leadership. In doing so, she's leaving a path of destruction in her wake. She has not maintained a balance on the scales of performance. As a result, she's harming the performance of her team and their partners, leading to subpar results. You have a leadership void on your hands.

Fortunately, you are part of an organization that has clearly defined what is expected of all leaders: balanced expectations between operational and human factors. Specific leadership behaviors have been identified and defined. Now, you have a choice. Do you continue to ignore or tolerate Lucille's behavior, hoping it will magically change? Or do you take steps to hold both yourself and her accountable for these expectations?

There are countless examples that could illustrate the leadership voids created when individuals and their leaders fail to maintain a balance between these two sides of the performance dynamic. You've likely encountered a few of your own. These voids can occur at any level of an organization and go unaddressed for days, weeks, or even years without accountability.

Once again, this is about adopting the heart and mind of Elevated Leadership and answering affirmatively to two key questions:

1. Am I willing to be an Elevated Leader, committed to leading myself and others to higher levels of success?
2. Am I willing to do what it takes to develop and increase my own and others' leadership capacity?

This journey begins on a personal level. When leadership falters at the individual level, it becomes nearly impossible to inspire a culture of leadership accountability throughout the organization. We must first hold ourselves to the commitments we make—both to ourselves and to others. When we identify a gap in our personal commitments, we must acknowledge it and address it swiftly to preserve our integrity.

We must also foster leadership accountability at the team level. It's crucial that every team member honors their leadership commitments. The same applies at the organizational level, where the executive leadership team should lead by example, upholding the same standards for themselves and others.

While this might seem daunting, it doesn't have to be. The process is straightforward: consistently communicate and reinforce expectations with clarity. Responsibility should be a shared value across the organization. When someone falls short, it's vital to address it promptly and constructively.

Some may argue that this level of responsibility is unrealistic, and perhaps they're right. However, I choose to focus on those who see the value in this approach—those who understand its transformative power. I've seen firsthand how a steadfast commitment to leadership can elevate performance at every level, driving both operational excellence and positive human outcomes. Imagine what would happen if everyone, from front-line employees to the CEO, were honestly held accountable for maintaining this balance.

> *"Sometimes, on the evening shift, tomorrow, this weekend, or next week, there is going to be a leadership void open up somewhere in this organization. It might be a problem to be solved, an improvement to be implemented, a relationship that needs repair, a customer or a team member that needs help. When it does, instead of waiting around or looking to someone else to lead, I encourage you to be the leader, pick it up, own it, and solve it. That's accountability. That's leadership anyone can practice."* —Jim the GM

Identify and Validate Your Leadership Voids

With the right Elevated Leadership mindset and heartset, a balanced approach to measuring inputs and results, and a culture of leadership accountability, the time is now to identify any leadership voids that may exist—whether in leading ourselves, others, or other leaders. This step is crucial for achieving elevation, requiring us to embody virtuous leadership qualities: honesty, humility, authenticity, and genuineness in our assessment. It also demands self-confidence and trust in our teams, understanding that having leadership voids is not a failure but a natural result of the constant change we face. The real failure lies in failing to acknowledge them or denying their existence. Without knowing where and what these voids are, we cannot address them effectively.

When identifying leadership voids, it is essential to look through the lens of E3C3 and the Six Core Elements, and from our own leadership perspective, whether we are leading ourselves, leading others and leading other leaders. We should inquire of ourselves how well and how frequently we are demonstrating the Six Core Elements, and their supporting competencies as outlined in the previous chapter. It is up to us and our teams to explore, discover, and identify where we might be falling short and in need of further development. Some of these voids may be obvious but, even more likely, not so obvious.

If we are honest with ourselves and each other, we already know of some leadership voids. Take a glance at the Six Core Elements: Embrace, Empower, Engage, Challenge and Coach. Make sure you understand what they truly mean. You may find some of the more obvious voids that exist, some personal, and some shared with other team members or many others in the organization.

We should ask ourselves: What are examples of situations where leadership was needed but went unmet? Acknowledging these instances is the first step toward filling these gaps.

Unknown Leadership Voids

Perhaps more important are the leadership voids we are not yet aware of but must discover. The most effective way to do this is through feedback. Sharing open and honest feedback with yourself and colleagues is crucial. Elevated Leaders need to know if there are leadership voids they should address. Think of your team as preparing to leave base camp for the summit; identifying any potential leadership voids that might hinder progress or pose safety risks is critically important to the entire team. It is important to make note of all feedback, even that which may be difficult to hear. Consider the source, assume good intent, and discern accordingly.

In addition to open and authentic personal feedback, a more structured approach, like leadership assessments, can be employed to discover unknown leadership voids. Depending on your purpose and your desired outcomes, I highly recommend using them. There are many excellent assessments available, far too many to mention. My top ten recommendations are included in the appendix (see Appendix I).

Regardless of other assessments used, you may want to consider the E3C3 Leadership Assessments for Leading Yourself, Leading Others, and Leading Other Leaders (see Appendix II–IV), which have been specifically tailored to assess a leader's effectiveness in demonstrating the Six Core Elements of Elevated Leadership and their supporting competencies.

It's also important to consider secondary indicators—good data that can help identify or validate these leadership voids and quantify their impact on your organization. Examples include employee engagement surveys, organizational assessments, program/project outcomes, and customer satisfaction, implementation rates, and other surveys. This can help to paint an even fuller picture and help balance the scales of performance.

Whatever methods you and your team use to identify leadership voids, it is critical to engage the entire organization in the process. Elevated Leadership is inclusive leadership. Everyone's input must be considered; every voice must be heard, and everyone must listen and take all perspectives seriously.

Finally, assess the output through the E3C3 lens to better understand these leadership voids. Once you've reached this point, you and your team are prepared to reach the summit. Now the hard work begins.

Implement E3C3: The Six Core Elements of Elevated Leadership

The cornerstone of leadership development is the individual development plan and process. At its core, leadership is a personal choice, and so is the commitment to developing one's leadership abilities. This is where the mindset and heartset of Elevated Leadership are truly tested—where the balance between performance and personal growth must be maintained, and where leadership accountability becomes paramount. Why? Because this is the challenging part. It's the moment when every leader must take responsibility for their own development and that of others, actively working to fill or prevent leadership voids.

The process starts by analyzing the data you've gathered, including feedback, assessment results, and other organizational metrics. In the context of E3C3, ask yourself: Which of the Six Core Elements are my strengths? Which are the strengths of our team and organization? Where are the opportunities for growth and improvement? Next, identify the specific Core Elements and Supporting Competencies you will commit to focusing on. This analysis forms the foundation and purpose of your personal development plan.

The 70-20-10 Development Framework

A solid and proven approach to personal development comes from the Center for Creative Leadership (CCL) in the form of the 70-20-10 Framework. This research-based, time-tested guideline for developing leaders emerged from over thirty years of CCL's Lessons of Experience research. According to the 70-20-10 rule, leaders develop through three types of experiences, allocated as follows:

- **70%** from challenging experiences and assignments
- **20%** from developmental relationships
- **10%** from coursework and training

This straightforward approach to individual development planning helps us strategically identify and prioritize our learning and development opportunities. Research shows that 70% of our development comes from our experiences and the lessons we glean from them, 20% stems from our relationships and interactions with others, and only 10% arises from formal coursework. By understanding this distribution, we can allocate our time and resources more effectively.

Through the lens of E3C3, the 70-20-10 Framework can be applied to address leadership voids and guide our development by answering key questions:

- **70%:** What specific actions can I take to cultivate the Six Core Elements?
- **20%:** Who should I collaborate with or learn from to elevate my performance?
- **10%:** What additional knowledge, skills, and formal learning do I need to reach the next level?

Referencing the Recommended Development Actions (Appendixes V – VII) can be particularly helpful in responding to these questions.

With your E3C3 development plan in place, you're ready to embark on the journey to the summit. You've embraced the mindset and heartset of an Elevated Leader, laid a strong foundation, and crafted a plan to guide you and your team to new heights. Now, it's time to take action and continue nurturing the leadership potential within yourself and others. That is what it means to practice Elevated Leadership.

CHAPTER FOURTEEN

Take Action

This Isn't Nuclear Physics!

I was facilitating a leadership development session one afternoon in Sandy, Utah, a charming suburb of Salt Lake City. The group consisted of thirty highly educated professionals—engineers, scientists, software engineers, and systems architects—who provided mission-critical safety technology for the nuclear power industry. Surrounded by such intellectual brainpower, I couldn't help but feel humbled; I even joked that my IQ might have gone up ten points just being there.

The group also included experienced mid-to-senior-level managers from various business units. For many, this was their first leadership development program. The topic for the afternoon session was "Having Difficult Conversations," a subject that resonates deeply with leaders because it's one of the biggest challenges they face.

As the session progressed, I had the participants dive into an exercise. They seemed unusually eager, likely because the topic was so relatable. Their task was to prepare for a difficult conversation, ideally one they had encountered in the past or might face soon. They would then practice the conversation in a role-play scenario with other team members, preparing them for real-life discussions.

As everyone got to work, reflecting and taking notes, I noticed one middle-aged gentleman, Ruben, showing signs of frustration. I approached him to see if he needed help, and he eagerly accepted my offer.

Ruben explained that the conversation he had in mind was particularly challenging: he needed to address a very personal issue related to one of his technicians, which had become a problem for the team. He had only been leading the team for less than a year and had never faced such a situation. I listened and probed for more details.

"Okay, can I ask what behavior you need to address?"

"It's his body odor. It's become a real problem for those he works with, and they've come to me for help," he explained.

"Those can be the toughest conversations," I said. "I suppose you're dreading it."

Ruben shrugged. "Well, yes," he replied.

I could see that Ruben was cooperative and eager to learn, so I suggested, "This is an excellent example of a difficult conversation that we can all relate to. Let's have the class take this one on together."

Ruben was more than happy to agree. "Whatever you all can do to help is fine with me!" he said, being a good sport about it.

We discussed the practice template as a group and developed a plan for addressing the issue positively. Eventually, we had Ruben participate in a role-play with another participant, practicing the conversation. The group was impressed with the approach.

When he finished, I asked Ruben if he felt better prepared for the conversation. "I suppose," he replied, only half-convincingly. "I'm going to give it a try."

One of his colleagues then shouted out, poking a little fun, "Ahh, come on, Ruben, this isn't nuclear physics. You've just got to go talk to the guy!"

Ruben laughed, appreciating the joke. "Yeah, I guess that's it. It's not nuclear physics. If it were, I'd feel a lot more comfortable." This brought a big chuckle from the group.

Suddenly, it hit me. Ruben, with all his years of experience as an accomplished scientist and several patented inventions to his credit, didn't necessarily see himself as a leader. I wondered how many others in the class felt the same way. It became clear that a leadership void had existed for some time but was only now being discovered. Ruben wasn't alone; others in the room were likely struggling with the same issue. Ruben was just brave enough to step up and share.

I tried to encourage him again. "I get it. You may think this isn't what you signed up for, but this is what leadership comes down to. Where others might shy away from this level of responsibility, leaders embrace it because they know it's the right thing to do. They see it, own it, and solve it."

Turning to the broader group, I said, "For all of us, the question is, 'Do I want to be a leader?' Because, as Ruben can attest, it's not always easy. Leadership requires us to continue developing ourselves and others, often stepping outside our comfort zones and doing what's challenging."

Ruben looked at me and said, "I don't think you could have said it any clearer."

I agreed, and then he stood up, grabbed his notebook and pen, shook my hand, and walked toward the door.

My heart sank—I had never had someone walk out on me during a leadership development session. But just before he exited, Ruben turned around with a big smile and returned to his seat. "Just kidding! I'm all in, Boss," he grinned. "I'm going to have that conversation with my guy next week. He deserves that much from me."

The entire class broke into laughter. Ruben sat there, grinning at me, and it finally dawned on me: the joke was on me. Ruben had just pulled off the most brilliant role-play exercise I had ever seen. The whole story about the teammate with body odor was an elaborate ruse, a role-play within a role-play, superbly acted by Ruben. All I could do was join in the laughs and appreciate the genius of the prank.

As the laughter died down, Ruben turned serious. "All kidding aside, this might have been a little prank, but it's not far from a real situation I have to deal with. I've never been in a leadership role, never thought of myself as a leader—an expert, sure; an engineer, yes; a teacher and professor, absolutely—but I never really thought about how important leadership and leadership development are until coming to this class. You know, this isn't nuclear physics. It's really about caring for people, making them your top priority, and working hard to develop them."

I stood in front of the group, nearly speechless, and then said, "Thanks, Ruben; I think you just summed it all up. That's a positive note to end the day on."

I will forever remember that session and the great participants we had. I'll also never forget Ruben and his quote: "This isn't nuclear physics; this is leadership!"

This experience perfectly illustrates the difference between those who answer the call to lead and those who might not, especially when faced with difficult situations. It was also clear that if Ruben had chosen not to lean into the problem as a leader, it would have left a significant leadership void for others. This is what leadership—and Elevated Leadership, in particular—is all about: leaning in from wherever you are to meet the challenge of being a leader and preventing these leadership voids from occurring in the first place. Ruben's example makes it easy to see the impact of answering the call to lead.

The E3C3 Leadership Experience

As Ruben pointed out, "This is not nuclear physics here." The true power of the Six Core Elements of Elevated Leadership lies in their simplicity, scalability, and positive impact on performance, engagement, and wellbeing. The methodology of E3C3 promotes active participation, full engagement, focused storytelling, active attention to the lessons learned, and actionable steps to put it all into practice, making the process simple yet profoundly impactful. It's about everyone doing a few simple things together with ever-increasing frequency and effectiveness. Taking this into consideration, I've provided the following, as a recommended approach toward implementing Elevated Leadership in your organization. I call it the Elevated Leadership Experience.

The E3C3 Experience is a structured learning and development journey facilitated by a certified E3C3 Guide and designed to immerse you in the Six Core Elements of Elevated Leadership. This journey unfolds through a series of stages, each building upon the last to create a cohesive and comprehensive leadership development process. The concepts are straightforward, with a strong focus on open, active engagement, sharing insights, and taking practical actions to elevate yourself and your team to higher levels of performance.

Your journey begins with Base Camp Orientation, progresses through the Ascent Mastermind, and culminates in the Summit Workshops—each phase carefully crafted to ensure maximum impact and long-term success.

Base Camp Orientation

Your journey starts with a concise ninety-minute, facilitated session designed to introduce you to E3C3: The Six Core Elements of Elevated Leadership. This session draws participants from all levels of the organization, providing a broad understanding of the E3C3 methodology. You'll gain insights into identifying leadership voids and reviewing feedback from your E3C3 Assessment (Appendixes II–IV). The session concludes with an overview of the Six Core Elements and the leadership competencies that support them. Once Base Camp is complete, you'll be prepared to embark on the next stage of your journey.

Ascent Mastermind

In the Ascent Mastermind, you join a group of like-minded individuals committed to mutual growth and leadership development. Together, you'll explore the concepts, methodologies, and philosophies of E3C3 Leadership in depth. In this four hour workshop guided by an E3C3 expert, you'll delve into the book's chapters, a few at a time, sharing your perspectives and experiences with the group. The emphasis on storytelling and lessons learned will help you identify practical steps for implementing E3C3 Leadership in your work and your daily life. By the end of the Ascent, you'll be ready to tackle the final leg of the journey: the Summit Workshops.

Summit Workshops

Reaching the summit requires a personalized approach. In these focused four hour workshops, you'll practice E3C3 Leadership from three critical perspectives: Leading Yourself, Leading Others, and Leading Other Leaders. As you advance through these sessions, you'll refine your leadership skills and apply the Six Core Elements in real-world scenarios.

Your participation in these workshops will not only enhance your own leadership abilities but also contribute to the overall success of your organization. Some participants may even choose to become certified E3C3 Guides themselves, helping to spread the principles of Elevated Leadership throughout the organization. As E3C3 takes root, you'll witness a measurable impact on performance, engagement, and well-being, laying a strong foundation for all future leadership development.

Reaching New Heights with E3C3 Leadership

As we come to the close of this journey, it's essential to reflect on the profound simplicity and power of the E3C3 framework. Leadership is not about complexity; it's about consistent action, mindful engagement, and a commitment to growth—both for oneself and for others. The Six Core Elements of Elevated Leadership—Embrace, Empower, Engage, Challenge, Coach, and Celebrate—serve as a roadmap for leaders at all levels, guiding them toward creating environments where people thrive and organizations excel.

Throughout this book, we've explored the transformative potential of these core elements. They are more than just principles; they are fundamental actionable strategies that, when practiced with intention by everyone, have the power to elevate leadership to new heights. By *embracing* the strengths and opportunities for growth within ourselves and others, by *empowering* our teams to take ownership of their roles, by *engaging* with purpose, by *challenging* the status quo, by *coaching* for continuous improvement, and by *celebrating* our experiences along the way, we lay the foundation for a leadership culture that is both dynamic and sustainable.

The journey of leadership is ongoing. With each summit gained the next one appears on the horizon. Each step taken reinforces the foundation for the next. As you implement the E3C3 methodology in your personal and professional life, remember that leadership is a collective effort. Everyone has a role to play. The impact of your leadership is magnified when everyone in your organization is aligned, engaged, and moving toward the same vision.

The true measure of leadership is not just in the milestones reached but in the growth experienced along the way. The E3C3 framework equips you to foster that growth—within yourself, your team, and your organization. As you continue to lead, may you do so with a sense of purpose, clarity, and a deep commitment to making a positive difference.

Thank you for embarking on this journey with me. The climb to Elevated Leadership is challenging, but the view from the summit is worth every step.

Keep climbing my friends. The view from the top is amazing! Let's go there together.

APPENDICES

APPENDIX I

Top Ten Leadership Development Assessments

Here are a few widely recognized and well-regarded leadership assessments that can provide valuable insights into leadership styles, competencies, and potential areas for development:

1. Center for Creative Leadership 360-Degree Feedback Assessment

Overview: This assessment gathers feedback on a leader's performance from multiple sources, including peers, subordinates, supervisors, and sometimes clients. It provides a comprehensive view of how the leader is perceived by others and identifies strengths and areas for improvement.

Best For: Leaders looking for a holistic understanding of their leadership impact, especially in team-based environments.

2. Myers-Briggs Type Indicator (MBTI)

Overview: The MBTI is a personality assessment that helps leaders understand their psychological preferences in how they perceive the world and make decisions. It categorizes individuals into 16 different personality types.

Best For: Leaders seeking to understand their personality type and how it affects their leadership style, decision-making, and interactions with others.

3. Emotional Intelligence (EQ) Assessment

Overview: This assessment measures a leader's ability to recognize, understand, and manage their own emotions and the emotions of others. High EQ is often linked to better leadership performance, especially in managing relationships and conflict.

Best For: Leaders who want to improve their interpersonal skills, empathy, and emotional management.

4. CliftonStrengths (formerly StrengthsFinder)

Overview: This assessment identifies an individual's top strengths out of 34 themes and helps leaders understand how to leverage their strengths to maximize their leadership potential.

Best For: Leaders interested in a strengths-based approach to leadership development, focusing on building on natural talents.

5. Leadership Practices Inventory (LPI)

Overview: Based on the Five Practices of Exemplary Leadership model by Kouzes and Posner, the LPI measures leadership behaviors and provides feedback on how frequently these behaviors are demonstrated by the leader.

Best For: Leaders looking to align their behaviors with proven leadership practices and enhance their effectiveness.

6. DISC Personality Assessment

Overview: The DISC assessment measures four primary personality traits: Dominance, Influence, Steadiness, and Conscientiousness. It helps leaders understand their behavior patterns and how they interact with others.

Best For: Leaders seeking to improve communication, teamwork, and productivity by understanding their own and others' behavioral styles.

7. Hogan Leadership Forecast Series

Overview: This series of assessments evaluates a leader's potential, challenges, and values, providing a comprehensive view of their strengths, weaknesses, and fit within organizational culture.

Best For: Leaders aiming for executive roles or those in high-stakes leadership positions, as it provides deep insights into leadership potential and derailers.

8. Situational Leadership II (SLII) Assessment

Overview: This assessment, based on Ken Blanchard's Situational Leadership Model, evaluates a leader's ability to adapt their leadership style to the needs of their team members based on their development level.

Best For: Leaders who need to adjust their leadership approach based on the situation and the readiness level of their followers.

9. The Leadership Circle Profile

Overview: This assessment combines leadership competencies with underlying thought patterns to provide a complete picture of a leader's strengths and areas for growth. It integrates feedback from both the leader and their colleagues.

Best For: Leaders who want a deep, integrated approach to personal and professional development.

10. E3C3 Self-Leadership Assessment (Appendix II–IV)

Overview: A custom assessment designed to help leaders evaluate their proficiency in the Six Core Elements of Elevated Leadership: Embrace, Empower, Engage, Challenge, Coach, and Celebrate. This tool provides insights into a leader's ability to lead themselves and others.

Best For: Leaders who follow the Elevated Leadership framework and want to align their development with its principles.

Each of these assessments has its unique strengths and can be chosen based on the specific needs and goals of the leader or organization.

APPENDIX II

E3C3 Self-Assessment: Leading Yourself

Introduction

Self-leadership is the foundation of effective leadership. Before you can lead others, you must be able to lead yourself with clarity, purpose, and integrity. The E3C3 Self-Assessment for Leading Yourself is designed to help you reflect on your personal leadership practices, evaluate your current competencies, and identify areas where you can grow. By assessing yourself across the six core elements of Elevated Leadership—Embrace, Empower, Engage, Challenge, Coach, and Celebrate—you will gain valuable insights into your strengths and areas for development, helping you to become the best version of yourself as a leader.

Instructions:

Rate yourself on the following statements using the scale provided below:

- 1 – Strongly Disagree
- 2 – Disagree
- 3 – Neutral
- 4 – Agree
- 5 – Strongly Agree

Section 1: Embrace

Self-Awareness

_____I regularly reflect on my emotions, strengths, and weaknesses to understand how they impact my behavior and decisions.

_____I am aware of how my actions affect others around me.

Authenticity

_____I stay true to my values and beliefs, even when faced with challenges or pressure.

_____My actions consistently reflect who I am and what I believe in.

Emotional Intelligence

_____I manage my emotions effectively, particularly in stressful situations.

_____I understand how my emotions influence my behavior and decision-making.

Integrity

_____I act consistently with my values, maintaining honesty and ethical behavior in all situations.

_____I make decisions that align with my moral principles, even when it is difficult.

Personal Accountability

_____I take full responsibility for my actions and their outcomes, whether they are positive or negative.

_____I hold myself accountable for the goals I set and the commitments I make.

Section 2: Empower

Self-Efficacy

_____I believe in my ability to achieve the goals I set for myself.
_____I approach challenges with confidence, knowing I can overcome them.

Goal Orientation

_____I set meaningful and challenging goals for myself regularly.
_____I am committed to achieving the goals I set, regardless of obstacles.

Initiative

_____I proactively seek opportunities to improve myself and accomplish tasks.
_____I take the lead in situations where action is required, rather than waiting for others.

Decision-Making

_____I make informed and timely decisions that align with my values and goals.
_____I consider the potential impact of my decisions on myself and others before acting.

Resilience

_____I bounce back from setbacks and stay focused on my objectives, even in difficult situations.
_____I view challenges as opportunities to grow and learn, rather than as obstacles.

Section 3: Engage

Motivation

_____I harness my inner drive to stay committed to my goals, even when facing challenges.
_____I regularly remind myself of the reasons behind my goals to maintain motivation.

Discipline

_____I maintain consistent effort and focus on my objectives, avoiding distractions.
_____I am able to stick to my plans and routines, even when it is difficult.

Focus

_____I stay attentive to my tasks and avoid distractions that could derail my progress.
_____I am able to concentrate on my goals, even in the face of competing demands.

Perseverance

_____I continue to strive toward my goals despite obstacles or difficulties.
_____I am persistent in pursuing my objectives, even when the path is tough.

Positive Attitude

_____I maintain an optimistic outlook, even in challenging situations.
_____I focus on solutions rather than dwelling on problems.

Section 4: Challenge

Adaptability

_____I am flexible and open to new experiences and changes.
_____I adjust my approach when faced with unexpected challenges or shifts in circumstances.

Risk-Taking

_____I am willing to step out of my comfort zone and embrace uncertainty.
_____I take calculated risks to pursue opportunities for growth and improvement.

Learning Agility

_____I continuously seek new knowledge and learning experiences to improve myself.
_____I apply lessons learned from past experiences to new situations and challenges.

Innovation

_____I embrace creativity and new ideas when solving problems.
_____I am open to exploring unconventional approaches to achieve my goals.

Resilience

_____I strengthen my ability to recover from challenges and bounce back stronger.
_____I remain determined and focused, even after experiencing setbacks.

Section 5: Coach

Self-Reflection

_____I regularly evaluate my performance and experiences to learn and improve.

_____I take time to reflect on my actions and their outcomes, identifying areas for growth.

Feedback Seeking

_____I actively seek input from others to enhance my growth and development.

_____I am open to receiving feedback and use it constructively to improve.

Growth Mindset

_____I believe that my abilities can be developed through effort and learning.

_____I embrace challenges and view them as opportunities to grow.

Continuous Learning

_____I pursue opportunities to develop new skills and knowledge.

_____I make a habit of learning from both successes and failures.

Performance Improvement

_____I focus on enhancing my effectiveness and achieving excellence in everything I do.

_____I regularly set and review personal performance goals to ensure continuous improvement.

Section 6: Celebrate

Self-Recognition

_____I acknowledge my achievements and progress, no matter how small.
_____I take pride in my accomplishments and celebrate milestones along the way.

Gratitude

_____I express appreciation for my efforts and successes.
_____I regularly practice gratitude, focusing on the positive aspects of my journey.

Positive Reinforcement

_____I encourage myself by celebrating small wins and progress toward my goals.
_____I use positive reinforcement to maintain motivation and momentum.

Self-Worth

_____I value my accomplishments and feel confident in my abilities.
_____I maintain a strong sense of self-worth, regardless of external validation.

Mindfulness

_____I practice being present and appreciating the journey, not just the outcomes.
_____I take time to reflect on and enjoy the process of achieving my goals.

Scoring the Assessment

- **Scoring:** Rate each statement on a scale of 1 to 5. Calculate the subtotal for each section by summing the points for all the questions in that section.
- **Overall Score:** Add the section totals for an overall score, with a maximum possible score of 300 points.

Interpreting the Scores

- **41-50 points per section: Highly Competent** – You are strong in this area and consistently demonstrate these competencies effectively.
- **31-40 points per section: Competent** – You have a solid grasp of these competencies but may have some areas for further development.
- **21-30 points per section: Developing** – You have some understanding of these competencies but should focus on growth in these areas.
- **11-20 points per section: Needs Improvement** – These competencies need significant attention and development.
- **0-10 points per section: Significant Development Needed** – There are substantial gaps that require focused development efforts.

This self-assessment is an essential tool for understanding where you stand in your personal leadership journey. By taking the time to reflect on your strengths and areas for growth, you're taking an important step toward becoming a more effective and self-aware leader. Use your results to build a focused action plan that will guide your ongoing development, helping you to reach your full potential and lead with confidence, authenticity, and purpose. Remember, self-leadership is the cornerstone of all leadership, and your commitment to continuous improvement will set the foundation for your future success.

APPENDIX III

E3C3 Self-Assessment: Leading Others

Introduction

Effective leadership is essential in fostering a high-performing team and driving success within an organization. As a leader, your ability to guide, inspire, and develop your team members significantly impacts their engagement, growth, and overall performance. The E3C3 Self-Assessment for Leading Others is designed to help you reflect on your leadership practices, assess your current competencies, and identify areas where you can further develop your skills. By evaluating yourself across the six core elements of Elevated Leadership—Embrace, Empower, Engage, Challenge, Coach, and Celebrate—you will gain a deeper understanding of your strengths and opportunities for growth in leading your team.

Instructions:

Rate yourself on the following statements using the scale provided below:

- 1 – Strongly Disagree
- 2 – Disagree
- 3 – Neutral
- 4 – Agree
- 5 – Strongly Agree

Section 1: Embrace

Inclusion

_____I actively seek out and value diverse perspectives within my team.
_____I create an environment where everyone feels included and respected.

Empathy

_____I make an effort to understand and appreciate the feelings and perspectives of my team members.
_____I consider the emotional and personal needs of my team when making decisions.

Cultural Competence

_____I recognize and respect cultural differences within my team.
_____I incorporate culturally relevant practices into my leadership approach.

Emotional Intelligence

_____I manage my emotions effectively when interacting with team members.
_____I respond appropriately to the emotional states of my team members.

Relationship Building

_____I invest time in developing strong, trust-based relationships with my team members.
_____I foster a positive and collaborative team environment through strong relationships.

Section 2: Empower

Delegation

_____I delegate significant responsibilities to team members to encourage ownership.
_____I trust my team members to make decisions independently.

Trust-Building

_____I establish and maintain trust within my team by empowering individuals.
_____I demonstrate trust in my team members through my actions and decisions.

Autonomy

_____I encourage my team members to take initiative in their work.
_____I give my team members the freedom to make decisions within their roles.

Motivating Others

_____I inspire my team members to take action and achieve their goals.
_____I regularly recognize and celebrate the accomplishments of my team.

Accountability

_____I hold myself and my team members accountable for our performance and outcomes.
_____I provide constructive feedback to help my team members grow and improve.

Section 3: Engage

Active Listening

_____I fully concentrate and respond to my team members' concerns and ideas.
_____I validate the input and feedback from my team members during discussions.

Communication

_____I clearly convey information to ensure understanding within my team.
_____I promote open and transparent communication among team members.

Collaboration

_____I foster teamwork and cooperative efforts among my team members.
_____I actively seek opportunities for collaboration within the team.

Feedback Seeking

_____I encourage my team members to share their thoughts and feedback openly.
_____I regularly seek feedback from my team to improve our collective performance.

Conflict Management

_____I address and resolve conflicts within my team in a constructive manner.
_____I use conflicts as opportunities for growth and improved team dynamics.

Section 4: Challenge

Goal Setting

_____I establish clear, challenging goals that motivate my team members.
_____I involve my team in the goal-setting process to ensure alignment and buy-in.

Performance Management

_____I monitor and manage the performance of my team to ensure continuous improvement.
_____I provide timely feedback and support to help my team meet performance expectations.

Innovation

_____I encourage creative thinking and the development of new ideas within my team.
_____I create an environment where innovation is valued and rewarded.

Resilience Building

_____I help my team members develop the ability to recover from setbacks and challenges.
_____I provide support and resources to build resilience within my team.

Talent Development

_____I identify and nurture the potential within my team members to help them grow.
_____I provide opportunities for professional development and skill-building.

Section 5: Coach

Mentoring

_____I provide guidance and share my expertise to help my team members develop.
_____I invest time in mentoring my team members to enhance their skills and capabilities.

Constructive Feedback

_____I offer feedback that is specific, actionable, and focused on improvement.
_____I create a feedback-rich environment where my team feels comfortable giving and receiving feedback.

Developmental Conversations

_____I engage in regular discussions focused on the personal and professional growth of my team members.
_____I help my team members set and achieve development goals through ongoing support.

Supportiveness

_____I am approachable and available to assist my team members with their challenges.
_____I actively listen and respond to the needs and concerns of my team members.

Empathy

_____I understand and address the unique developmental needs of each team member.
_____I tailor my coaching approach to meet the individual needs of my team members.

Section 6: Celebrate

Recognition

_____I regularly acknowledge the achievements and contributions of my team members.

_____I celebrate successes, both big and small, to reinforce positive behavior.

Positive Reinforcement

_____I use positive reinforcement to encourage desired behaviors within my team.

_____I ensure that recognition and reinforcement are a regular part of my leadership practice.

Appreciation

_____I express gratitude for the efforts and contributions of my team members.

_____I create an environment where team members feel valued and appreciated.

Team Spirit

_____I foster a sense of camaraderie and collective pride within my team.

_____I encourage team members to support and celebrate each other's successes.

Motivation

_____I use celebration and recognition to keep my team motivated and engaged.

_____I help my team members see the connection between their efforts and the team's success.

Scoring the Assessment

- **Scoring:** As with the Leading Other Leaders assessment, score each response from 1 to 5.
- **Section Scores:** Add up the scores for each section to get a total for each core element.
- **Overall Score:** Add the section totals for an overall score, with the maximum possible score being 300 points.

Interpreting the Scores

- **41–50 points per section: Highly Competent** – You are strong in this area and consistently demonstrate these competencies effectively.
- **31–40 points per section: Competent** – You have a solid grasp of these competencies but may have some areas for further development.
- **21–30 points per section: Developing** – You have some understanding of these competencies but should focus on growth in these areas.
- **11–20 points per section: Needs Improvement** – These competencies need significant attention and development.
- **0–10 points per section: Significant Development Needed** – There are substantial gaps that require focused development efforts.

Action Plan

After scoring, create an action plan:

- **High Scores:** Identify how you can leverage your strengths in your leadership role.
- **Mid-range Scores:** Set goals to refine and enhance your skills.
- **Low Scores:** Focus on specific areas where improvement is needed and seek out resources, training, or mentorship to help you grow.

Upon completing this self-assessment, take some time to reflect on your scores and what they reveal about your leadership style. Use this tool as a guide to creating a targeted action plan that leverages your strengths and addresses areas for improvement. Leadership is a continuous journey of learning and development, and by committing to enhancing your skills, you not only grow as a leader but also contribute to the success and well-being of your team. Remember, the most effective leaders are those who invest in their own growth and the growth of others, fostering a culture of continuous improvement and excellence.

APPENDIX IV

E3C3 Self-Assessment: Leading Other Leaders

Introduction

Leadership is not just about managing tasks and people; it's about inspiring others, fostering growth, and building a strong, cohesive team. As a leader of other leaders, your role is pivotal in shaping the culture, vision, and success of your organization. The E3C3 Self-Assessment for Leading Other Leaders is designed to help you reflect on your leadership practices and identify areas where you excel as well as opportunities for growth. By honestly assessing your competencies across the six core elements of Elevated Leadership—Embrace, Empower, Engage, Challenge, Coach, and Celebrate—you will gain valuable insights into your strengths and areas where you can enhance your effectiveness.

Instructions:

Rate yourself on the following statements using the scale provided below:

- 1 – Strongly Disagree
- 2 – Disagree
- 3 – Neutral
- 4 – Agree
- 5 – Strongly Agree

Section 1: Embrace

Inclusion

_____I actively seek out and value diverse perspectives when making decisions.

_____I create an inclusive environment where all leaders feel respected and valued.

Visionary Thinking

_____I can articulate a clear and inspiring vision for the organization that aligns with our values.

_____I encourage other leaders to contribute to and support our shared vision.

Strategic Relationship Building

_____I invest time in building strong relationships with other leaders in the organization.

_____I leverage these relationships to foster collaboration and achieve our strategic goals.

Emotional Intelligence

_____I understand and manage my emotions effectively in leadership situations.

_____I recognize and manage the emotions of others in leadership situations to maintain a positive and productive environment.

Cultural Competence

_____I recognize and respect cultural differences within my leadership team.

_____I incorporate culturally relevant practices into my leadership approach.

Section 2: Empower

Delegation

_____I confidently delegate significant responsibilities to other leaders.
_____I trust other leaders to make decisions and take ownership of their work.

Empowerment

_____I provide the autonomy needed for leaders to make decisions within their roles.
_____I encourage other leaders to take initiative and innovate.

Trust-Building

_____I am transparent and consistent in my actions, which helps build trust with other leaders.
_____I demonstrate trust in the leaders I work with by giving them the authority to act.

Accountability

_____I hold myself and other leaders accountable for our performance and decisions.
_____I provide constructive feedback to help other leaders grow and improve.

Motivating Others

_____I recognize and leverage the intrinsic motivators of other leaders.
_____I consistently inspire and encourage leaders to perform at their best.

Section 3: Engage

Communication

_____I facilitate open and transparent communication with other leaders.
_____I ensure that all voices are heard and considered in decision-making processes.

Active Listening

_____I actively listen to the ideas and concerns of other leaders.
_____I validate and incorporate feedback from other leaders into my decision-making.

Collaboration

_____I promote teamwork and cooperation among the leaders I work with.
_____I actively seek opportunities for collaboration across different teams or departments.

Feedback Seeking

_____I regularly seek feedback from other leaders on my performance and decisions.
_____I encourage an environment where feedback is shared openly and constructively.

Conflict Resolution

_____I effectively address and resolve conflicts between leaders in a fair and timely manner.
_____I use conflicts as opportunities for growth and improved understanding among leaders.

Section 4: Challenge

Talent Development

_____I identify and nurture the potential within other leaders, helping them grow.
_____I provide opportunities for leaders to stretch their abilities and take on new challenges.

Strategic Thinking

_____I challenge other leaders to think critically about long-term goals and strategies.
_____I encourage innovation and creative thinking among the leadership team.

Change Leadership

_____I effectively lead other leaders through organizational change, fostering adaptability.
_____I help leaders embrace new challenges and view them as opportunities for growth.

Performance Management

_____I set high expectations for leaders and provide the necessary support to achieve them.
_____I regularly review and provide feedback on the performance of other leaders.

Innovation

_____I challenge leaders to think creatively and explore new approaches to solving problems.
_____I create an environment where innovative ideas are encouraged and valued.

Section 5: Coach

Strategic Mentorship

_____I provide guidance to other leaders that aligns with our organization's strategy.
_____I help other leaders navigate complex challenges by offering high-level mentorship.

Leadership Development

_____I actively work on developing the leadership capabilities of others.
_____I prepare leaders for higher levels of responsibility through targeted development efforts.

Systems Thinking

_____I coach leaders to understand the interdependencies within the organization.
_____I encourage leaders to think in terms of systems and processes when making decisions.

Executive Presence

_____I help other leaders develop the communication and presence needed to influence at the highest levels.
_____I provide feedback to leaders on how to enhance their executive presence.

Succession Planning

_____I guide leaders in identifying and developing potential successors.
_____I work with leaders to create and implement effective succession plans.

Section 6: Celebrate

Recognition

_____I regularly acknowledge the achievements and contributions of other leaders.
_____I create opportunities to publicly recognize and celebrate the successes of leaders.

Appreciation

_____I express gratitude for the efforts of other leaders, fostering a positive work environment.
_____I ensure that leaders feel valued and appreciated for their contributions.

Public Acknowledgment

_____I make a point to celebrate the successes of leaders in visible ways.
_____I use public acknowledgment to inspire others and build morale within the leadership team.

Team Spirit

_____I promote a sense of camaraderie and collective pride among leaders.
_____I encourage leaders to support and celebrate each other's successes.

Positive Reinforcement

_____I use celebration as a tool to reinforce desired behaviors and outcomes among leaders.
_____I ensure that positive reinforcement is a regular part of our leadership culture.

Scoring the Assessment

- **Scoring:** Rate each statement on a scale of 1 to 5. Calculate the subtotal for each section by summing the points for all the questions in that section.
- **Overall Score:** Add the section totals for an overall score, with a maximum possible score of 300 points.

Interpreting the Scores

- **41–50 points per section: Highly Competent** – You are strong in this area and consistently demonstrate these competencies effectively.
- **31–40 points per section: Competent** – You have a solid grasp of these competencies but may have some areas for further development.
- **21–30 points per section: Developing** – You have some understanding of these competencies but should focus on growth in these areas.
- **11–20 points per section: Needs Improvement** – These competencies need significant attention and development.
- **0–10 points per section: Significant Development Needed** – There are substantial gaps that require focused development efforts.

Upon completing this self-assessment, take some time to reflect on your scores in each section. This reflection is an opportunity to celebrate your strengths and to identify areas where you can grow as a leader. Use this assessment as a starting point for your personal development journey, setting specific goals for improvement and seeking out resources, training, or mentorship to help you achieve them. Remember, leadership is a continuous process of learning and growth, and your commitment to developing your skills will not only benefit you but also the leaders you guide and the organization you serve.

APPENDIX V

Recommended Development Actions: Leading Yourself with E3C3

Leading Yourself is the cornerstone of the E3C3 framework and serves as the foundation for your growth as a leader. By focusing on the core elements—Embrace, Empower, and Engage—you strengthen your ability to lead with authenticity, build confidence, and maintain resilience. These developmental actions are designed to enhance self-awareness, accountability, and motivation, ensuring that you continuously improve both personally and professionally. As you embrace your values, empower yourself through decisive action, and stay engaged with discipline and perseverance, you pave the way for success in all areas of your life.

Section 1: Embrace

Self-Awareness

- **Developmental Action 1:** Keep a daily journal to reflect on your emotions, strengths, and areas for improvement, noting how they impact your decisions and interactions.
- **Developmental Action 2:** Engage in regular self-assessment exercises or seek feedback from a trusted mentor or coach to gain deeper insights into your behavior and its effects on others.

Authenticity

- **Developmental Action 1:** Identify your core values and ensure your decisions and actions consistently align with these values, even under pressure.
- **Developmental Action 2:** Practice transparency by openly sharing your thoughts and feelings in appropriate situations, staying true to who you are.

Emotional Intelligence

- **Developmental Action 1:** Participate in an emotional intelligence workshop to enhance your ability to recognize and manage your emotions effectively.
- **Developmental Action 2:** Practice mindfulness techniques to become more aware of your emotional triggers and responses, and how they influence your behavior.

Integrity

- **Developmental Action 1:** Regularly review your decisions and actions to ensure they align with your personal values and ethical standards, making adjustments as necessary.
- **Developmental Action 2:** Commit to honesty and ethical behavior in all your interactions, even when it may be challenging, and hold yourself accountable to this standard.

Personal Accountability

- **Developmental Action 1:** Set clear personal and professional goals, and track your progress regularly, holding yourself accountable for the outcomes.
- **Developmental Action 2:** When mistakes occur, take full responsibility and focus on finding solutions rather than assigning blame or making excuses.

Section 2: Empower

Self-Efficacy

- **Developmental Action 1:** Set small, achievable goals to build confidence in your ability to succeed and gradually take on larger challenges.
- **Developmental Action 2:** Reflect on past successes and accomplishments to reinforce your belief in your abilities and to boost your self-confidence.

Goal Orientation

- **Developmental Action 1:** Break down long-term goals into smaller, manageable steps and create a timeline for achieving them, reviewing your progress regularly.
- **Developmental Action 2:** Use goal-setting frameworks like SMART (Specific, Measurable, Achievable, Relevant, Time-bound) to ensure your goals are clear and actionable.

Initiative

- **Developmental Action 1:** Identify areas in your work or personal life where you can take proactive steps and begin taking action without waiting for external prompts.
- **Developmental Action 2:** Volunteer for new challenges or projects that align with your goals and interests, demonstrating leadership and initiative.

Decision-Making

- **Developmental Action 1:** Practice making decisions by gathering relevant information, considering the pros and cons and evaluating potential outcomes before taking action.
- **Developmental Action 2:** Reflect on past decisions to learn from the outcomes, identifying what worked well and what could be improved in your decision-making process.

Resilience

- **Developmental Action 1:** Develop coping strategies, such as mindfulness or stress management techniques, to help you stay focused and positive during challenging times.
- **Developmental Action 2:** Reframe setbacks as learning opportunities, focusing on what you can gain from the experience rather than dwelling on the difficulties.

Section 3: Engage

Motivation

- **Developmental Action 1:** Identify what drives you and create a personal mission statement that reflects your core motivations, referring to it regularly to stay focused.
- **Developmental Action 2:** Set personal rewards for achieving milestones to maintain motivation and acknowledge your progress.

Discipline

- **Developmental Action 1:** Establish a daily routine that supports your goals, incorporating regular time for focused work and self-care.
- **Developmental Action 2:** Use time management tools to prioritize tasks and ensure you stay on track, minimizing distractions and maintaining focus.

Focus

- **Developmental Action 1:** Create a distraction-free work environment by setting boundaries and specific times for deep work.
- **Developmental Action 2:** Practice mindfulness or meditation to improve your ability to concentrate and stay present in the moment.

Perseverance

- **Developmental Action 1:** Break down large tasks into smaller, manageable steps to avoid feeling overwhelmed and to keep moving forward.
- **Developmental Action 2:** Reflect on past challenges you have overcome to remind yourself of your resilience and ability to persevere through difficult times.

Positive Attitude

- **Developmental Action 1:** Begin each day with a gratitude practice, focusing on what you are thankful for and maintaining a positive outlook throughout the day.
- **Developmental Action 2:** Surround yourself with positive influences, such as mentors, colleagues, or inspirational content, to help maintain an optimistic mindset.

Section 4: Challenge

Adaptability

- **Developmental Action 1:** Embrace change by actively seeking out new experiences and learning opportunities that push you out of your comfort zone.
- **Developmental Action 2:** Practice adjusting your approach in real-time when faced with unexpected challenges, staying flexible and open to new solutions.

Risk-Taking

- **Developmental Action 1:** Identify areas where you can take calculated risks and step out of your comfort zone, and take action on those opportunities.
- **Developmental Action 2:** Reflect on the outcomes of past risks to learn from the experience, and use these insights to inform future risk-taking decisions.

Learning Agility

- **Developmental Action 1:** Continuously seek new knowledge by attending workshops, reading books, or engaging in online courses that challenge your thinking.
- **Developmental Action 2:** Apply the lessons learned from past experiences to new situations, demonstrating your ability to learn and adapt quickly.

Innovation

- **Developmental Action 1:** Set aside regular time for creative thinking and brainstorming sessions where you can explore new ideas and solutions.
- **Developmental Action 2:** Experiment with unconventional approaches to problem-solving, embracing creativity and innovation in your personal and professional life.

Resilience

- **Developmental Action 1:** Build resilience by practicing stress management techniques such as deep breathing, meditation, or physical exercise.
- **Developmental Action 2:** Reflect on how you have overcome past challenges to strengthen your ability to bounce back from future setbacks.

Section 5: Coach

Self-Reflection

- **Developmental Action 1:** Schedule regular time for self-reflection to evaluate your actions, decisions, and areas for improvement, using a reflection journal to document your thoughts.
- **Developmental Action 2:** Conduct regular personal performance reviews, setting aside time to assess your progress and identify areas for growth.

Feedback Seeking

- **Developmental Action 1:** Actively seek feedback from trusted colleagues, mentors, or peers to gain insights into your strengths and areas for development.
- **Developmental Action 2:** Implement the feedback you receive by creating an action plan and tracking your progress over time.

Growth Mindset

- **Developmental Action 1:** Embrace challenges as opportunities to grow by setting stretch goals that push you beyond your current capabilities.
- **Developmental Action 2:** Regularly remind yourself that your abilities can be developed through effort and learning, and seek out new learning opportunities.

Continuous Learning

- **Developmental Action 1:** Pursue ongoing learning opportunities, such as online courses, workshops, or seminars, to continually develop new skills and knowledge.
- **Developmental Action 2:** Create a personal development plan that includes specific learning goals and milestones, reviewing it regularly to track your progress.

Performance Improvement

- **Developmental Action 1:** Set specific performance goals for yourself, and regularly review your progress toward achieving them, adjusting as necessary.
- **Developmental Action 2:** Seek out resources, such as books, courses, or mentors that can help you improve your effectiveness and achieve excellence in your personal and professional life.

Section 6: Celebrate

Self-Recognition

- **Developmental Action 1:** Regularly acknowledge your achievements and progress, no matter how small, and take pride in your accomplishments.
- **Developmental Action 2:** Celebrate milestones by rewarding yourself with something meaningful that acknowledges your hard work.

Gratitude

- **Developmental Action 1:** Practice daily gratitude by reflecting on the positive aspects of your life and acknowledging your efforts and successes.
- **Developmental Action 2:** Express appreciation for the support you receive from others, and recognize how it contributes to your achievements.

Positive Reinforcement

- **Developmental Action 1:** Use positive reinforcement to encourage yourself by celebrating small wins and progress toward your goals.
- **Developmental Action 2:** Set up a system of rewards, such as treating yourself to something enjoyable, to maintain motivation and momentum.

Self-Worth

- **Developmental Action 1:** Regularly remind yourself of your accomplishments and the value you bring to your personal and professional life, reinforcing your self-worth.
- **Developmental Action 2:** Practice self-compassion by treating yourself with kindness and understanding, especially during challenging times.

Mindfulness

- **Developmental Action 1:** Practice mindfulness techniques, such as meditation or deep breathing, to stay present and focused on the moment, appreciating the journey as much as the outcome.
- **Developmental Action 2:** Take time to reflect on and enjoy the process of achieving your goals, not just the results, fostering a deeper sense of fulfillment.

Incorporating these developmental actions strengthens your ability to embrace authenticity, empower growth, and engage with focus and resilience, all aligned with the E3C3: The Six Core Elements of Elevated Leadership. By committing to self-awareness, personal accountability, and goal setting, you build a solid foundation for continuous improvement. Empowering yourself through initiative and decision-making, while staying engaged with discipline and a positive attitude, ensures lasting progress and success in both personal and professional leadership.

APPENDIX VI

Recommended Development Actions: Leading Others with E3C3

Leading Others is a critical component of the E3C3 framework, and it involves cultivating a leadership approach that fosters inclusion, empathy, trust, and empowerment. By embracing diverse perspectives, empowering team members through delegation and autonomy, and engaging them with clear communication and accountability, leaders can create an environment where individuals and teams can thrive. The developmental actions outlined here are designed to enhance these competencies, enabling leaders to build strong relationships, motivate their teams, and drive sustained success within their organizations.

Section 1: Embrace

Inclusion

- **Developmental Action 1:** Actively seek out and include diverse perspectives in team discussions and decision-making processes to ensure all voices are heard.
- **Developmental Action 2:** Participate in workshops or training on diversity and inclusion to enhance your understanding and skills in creating an inclusive team environment.

Empathy

- **Developmental Action 1:** Practice active listening during conversations with team members, making a conscious effort to understand their emotions and perspectives.
- **Developmental Action 2:** Regularly check in with team members on a personal level to better understand their motivations, challenges, and concerns.

Cultural Competence

- **Developmental Action 1:** Learn about the cultural backgrounds of your team members and incorporate culturally relevant practices into your leadership approach.
- **Developmental Action 2:** Engage in cross-cultural training to increase your awareness and ability to manage cultural differences effectively within your team.

Emotional Intelligence

- **Developmental Action 1:** Reflect on your emotional responses in different leadership situations and identify areas where you could better manage your emotions.
- **Developmental Action 2:** Solicit feedback from peers on how your emotions impact your leadership style, and work on areas for improvement based on this feedback.

Relationship Building

- **Developmental Action 1:** Schedule regular one-on-one meetings with team members to build rapport, trust, and understanding.
- **Developmental Action 2:** Participate in team-building activities to strengthen relationships and foster a positive, collaborative team environment.

Section 2: Empower

Delegation

- **Developmental Action 1:** Identify tasks that can be delegated to team members and create a plan to empower them to take ownership and responsibility.
- **Developmental Action 2:** Provide clear instructions and follow-up to ensure successful delegation, offering support and guidance as needed.

Trust-Building

- **Developmental Action 1:** Be transparent with your team about decisions, challenges, and changes, fostering an environment of trust and openness.
- **Developmental Action 2:** Demonstrate reliability by consistently following through on your commitments and encouraging the same level of accountability in others.

Autonomy

- **Developmental Action 1:** Encourage team members to take initiative by giving them the freedom to make decisions within their roles, empowering them to lead.
- **Developmental Action 2:** Create a safe environment where team members feel comfortable taking risks and learning from their experiences without fear of failure.

Motivating Others

- **Developmental Action 1:** Identify the intrinsic motivators for each team member and tailor your leadership approach to align with their individual drivers and goals.
- **Developmental Action 2:** Regularly recognize and celebrate both small and large achievements to maintain high levels of motivation and morale within your team.

Accountability

- **Developmental Action 1:** Set clear expectations for your team and hold team members accountable for their performance, providing constructive feedback as needed.
- **Developmental Action 2:** Implement regular performance reviews to track progress, address any areas of concern, and reinforce accountability.

Section 3: Engage

Active Listening

- **Developmental Action 1:** Practice active listening by fully concentrating on what team members are saying during meetings and by responding thoughtfully to their concerns and ideas.
- **Developmental Action 2:** Validate and incorporate feedback from team members during discussions, ensuring they feel heard and valued.

Communication

- **Developmental Action 1:** Improve communication clarity by providing concise and clear instructions and by ensuring that all team members understand their roles and responsibilities.
- **Developmental Action 2:** Promote open and transparent communication by encouraging team members to share their thoughts and feedback openly during meetings and discussions.

Collaboration

- **Developmental Action 1:** Foster teamwork by creating opportunities for cross-functional projects where team members can collaborate and share ideas.
- **Developmental Action 2:** Use collaborative tools and platforms to improve teamwork and communication within your team, ensuring that everyone is aligned with the team's goals.

Feedback Seeking

- **Developmental Action 1:** Regularly ask team members for feedback on your leadership approach and decision-making processes, demonstrating that you value their input.
- **Developmental Action 2:** Create an anonymous feedback mechanism to encourage honest and open feedback from team members, which can be used to improve team dynamics.

Conflict Management

- **Developmental Action 1:** Address conflicts within the team promptly and constructively, focusing on finding mutually agreeable solutions that strengthen team dynamics.
- **Developmental Action 2:** Provide conflict resolution training for your team to equip them with the skills to handle disagreements effectively and maintain a positive work environment.

Section 4: Challenge

Goal Setting

- **Developmental Action 1:** Collaborate with your team to set clear, challenging goals that align with the team's overall objectives, ensuring that each member is motivated and committed to achieving them.
- **Developmental Action 2:** Regularly review and adjust goals with your team to ensure they remain relevant and motivating, and that everyone is aligned with the desired outcomes.

Performance Management

- **Developmental Action 1:** Implement a performance management system that includes regular feedback, coaching, and development opportunities for all team members.
- **Developmental Action 2:** Hold regular performance review sessions with team members to discuss their progress, address any areas of concern, and provide support for continuous improvement.

Innovation

- **Developmental Action 1:** Encourage creative thinking within your team by setting aside time for brainstorming sessions where team members can propose new ideas and solutions.
- **Developmental Action 2:** Reward innovative ideas and solutions that improve team performance or processes, fostering a culture of innovation and continuous improvement.

Resilience Building

- **Developmental Action 1:** Help team members develop resilience by providing support during challenging times and encouraging them to view setbacks as learning opportunities.
- **Developmental Action 2:** Offer training on stress management and resilience to help your team cope with challenges and maintain a positive, productive work environment.

Talent Development

- **Developmental Action 1:** Identify the strengths and development needs of each team member, and create individual development plans to help them grow and reach their full potential.
- **Developmental Action 2:** Provide opportunities for team members to take on new roles or projects that challenge them and build their skills, preparing them for future leadership roles.

Section 5: Coach

Mentoring

- **Developmental Action 1:** Actively mentor team members by sharing your expertise and providing guidance on their career development and professional growth.
- **Developmental Action 2:** Pair experienced team members with less experienced ones for peer mentoring, fostering knowledge sharing and development within the team.

Constructive Feedback

- **Developmental Action 1:** Provide timely, specific, and actionable feedback that helps team members improve their performance and develop new skills.
- **Developmental Action 2:** Create a feedback-rich environment where team members feel comfortable giving and receiving feedback from their peers and from you as their leader.

Developmental Conversations

- **Developmental Action 1:** Schedule regular one-on-one meetings with team members to discuss their career goals and how you can support their development.
- **Developmental Action 2:** Use development planning tools to help team members set and achieve personal and professional goals, providing ongoing support and guidance.

Supportiveness

- **Developmental Action 1:** Be approachable and make yourself available to assist team members with challenges, offering guidance and resources as needed to help them succeed.
- **Developmental Action 2:** Foster a supportive team environment by recognizing and addressing individual needs and concerns, ensuring that each team member feels valued and supported.

Empathy

- **Developmental Action 1:** Show empathy by actively listening to team members' concerns and offering support when they face personal or professional challenges.
- **Developmental Action 2:** Tailor your coaching and leadership approach to meet the unique needs of each team member, demonstrating an understanding of their individual circumstances.

Section 6: Celebrate

Recognition

- **Developmental Action 1:** Regularly acknowledge and celebrate the achievements and contributions of team members, both individually and as a group.
- **Developmental Action 2:** Implement a recognition program that highlights and rewards outstanding performance and teamwork within your team.

Positive Reinforcement

- **Developmental Action 1:** Use positive reinforcement to encourage desired behaviors and performance within your team, praising team members when they meet or exceed expectations.
- **Developmental Action 2:** Provide immediate positive feedback to reinforce behaviors that contribute to team success, making recognition a regular part of your leadership practice.

Appreciation

- **Developmental Action 1:** Express gratitude regularly for the hard work and dedication of your team members, both privately and publicly.
- **Developmental Action 2:** Create opportunities for team members to express appreciation for each other's contributions, fostering a positive and collaborative team environment.

Team Spirit

- **Developmental Action 1:** Organize team-building activities that promote camaraderie, mutual support, and a sense of collective pride among team members.
- **Developmental Action 2:** Celebrate team successes together, reinforcing the importance of working collaboratively to achieve common goals.

Motivation

- **Developmental Action 1:** Use celebration and recognition to keep your team motivated and engaged, particularly after completing major projects or overcoming challenges.
- **Developmental Action 2:** Help team members see the connection between their efforts and the overall success of the team, reinforcing their sense of purpose and motivation.

Incorporating these developmental actions for Leading Others fosters trust, inclusion, and accountability. By embracing diversity, empowering team members, and engaging with empathy and clear communication, leaders unlock their teams' potential. The E3C3 framework's Six Core Elements—Embrace, Empower, Engage, Challenge, Coach, and Celebrate—guide leaders in building cohesive teams that overcome challenges and succeed. By focusing on relationships and supporting growth, leaders create a culture where everyone thrives and contributes to the organization's success.

APPENDIX VII

Recommended Development Actions: Leading Other Leaders with E3C3

Leading Other Leaders is a vital aspect of the E3C3 framework, focusing on empowering leaders to drive performance and inspire their teams. By embracing inclusive leadership, fostering emotional intelligence, and building strategic relationships, leaders can create a collaborative and supportive environment. These developmental actions are designed to help leaders delegate effectively, build trust, and challenge others to grow while maintaining accountability. Through coaching and celebrating successes, leaders can reinforce positive behaviors and ensure that the leadership team remains motivated and aligned with the organization's vision. These actions create a culture of continuous improvement and long-term success.

Section 1: Embrace

Inclusion

- **Developmental Action 1:** Facilitate inclusive leadership training for all leaders in your team to ensure everyone values and promotes diversity.
- **Developmental Action 2:** Lead by example by making inclusivity a key part of your leadership style, encouraging others to seek out and value diverse perspectives.

Visionary Thinking

- **Developmental Action 1:** Organize strategic planning sessions with other leaders to align on the long-term vision and direction of the organization.
- **Developmental Action 2:** Encourage leaders to think creatively and propose innovative ideas that align with the organizational vision, fostering a shared sense of purpose.

Strategic Relationship Building

- **Developmental Action 1:** Invest time in building strong relationships with other leaders within the organization to enhance collaboration and trust.
- **Developmental Action 2:** Attend industry events or networking opportunities to expand your professional network and bring new insights to your team.

Emotional Intelligence

- **Developmental Action 1:** Offer emotional intelligence training to leaders, emphasizing the importance of understanding and managing emotions in leadership.
- **Developmental Action 2:** Model emotionally intelligent behavior by remaining calm and composed during stressful situations, setting an example for other leaders.

Cultural Competence

- **Developmental Action 1:** Encourage leaders to participate in cross-cultural exchanges or projects to increase their cultural competence and global perspective.
- **Developmental Action 2:** Implement diversity and inclusion initiatives that promote cultural awareness and understanding within the leadership team.

Section 2: Empower

Delegation

- **Developmental Action 1:** Delegate high-impact projects to other leaders, giving them the opportunity to demonstrate their leadership capabilities.
- **Developmental Action 2:** Provide clear guidance and support while allowing leaders the autonomy to execute projects as they see fit, fostering ownership and accountability.

Empowerment

- **Developmental Action 1:** Foster a culture of empowerment by encouraging leaders to take ownership of their decisions and initiatives.
- **Developmental Action 2:** Support leaders in developing their teams by giving them the resources and autonomy needed to succeed.

Trust-Building

- **Developmental Action 1:** Encourage transparency and open communication among leaders to build a strong foundation of trust within the leadership team.
- **Developmental Action 2:** Demonstrate trust in other leaders by giving them the authority and autonomy to make critical decisions, and by consistently supporting their judgment.

Accountability

- **Developmental Action 1:** Hold leaders accountable for their team's performance and outcomes, providing constructive feedback and guidance as needed.
- **Developmental Action 2:** Establish clear goals and expectations for leaders, and regularly review their progress to ensure they are meeting organizational objectives.

Motivating Others

- **Developmental Action 1:** Recognize and reward leaders who demonstrate strong performance and contribute to the organization's success.
- **Developmental Action 2:** Create a motivational culture by setting challenging but achievable goals for leaders and supporting their efforts to meet them.

Section 3: Engage

Communication

- **Developmental Action 1:** Facilitate open and transparent communication channels with other leaders, ensuring that important information flows freely and efficiently.
- **Developmental Action 2:** Encourage leaders to share their ideas and feedback openly, creating a collaborative decision-making environment where all voices are heard.

Active Listening

- **Developmental Action 1:** Practice active listening during leadership meetings, fully concentrating on what other leaders are saying and validating their input.
- **Developmental Action 2:** Incorporate feedback from other leaders into your decision-making processes, demonstrating that their opinions are valued and considered.

Collaboration

- **Developmental Action 1:** Promote a culture of teamwork among leaders by encouraging cross-functional collaboration and the sharing of best practices.
- **Developmental Action 2:** Create opportunities for leaders to collaborate on projects that require diverse skill sets, fostering cooperation and innovation.

Feedback Seeking

- **Developmental Action 1:** Regularly seek feedback from other leaders on your performance and decision-making, using this input to refine your leadership approach.
- **Developmental Action 2:** Create an environment where feedback is shared openly and constructively, encouraging leaders to provide input that drives continuous improvement.

Conflict Resolution

- **Developmental Action 1:** Address conflicts between leaders promptly and impartially, focusing on finding resolutions that benefit the organization as a whole.
- **Developmental Action 2:** Use conflicts as learning opportunities, helping leaders understand different perspectives and grow from the experience.

Section 4: Challenge

Talent Development

- **Developmental Action 1:** Identify high-potential leaders within your team and create tailored development plans to help them reach their full potential.
- **Developmental Action 2:** Provide opportunities for leaders to take on stretch assignments that challenge their abilities and prepare them for greater responsibilities.

Strategic Thinking

- **Developmental Action 1:** Encourage leaders to engage in long-term strategic planning, helping them develop the ability to think critically about the future of the organization.
- **Developmental Action 2:** Facilitate strategic thinking workshops or retreats where leaders can collaborate on developing innovative solutions to complex challenges.

Change Leadership

- **Developmental Action 1:** Lead by example during times of change, demonstrating adaptability and a positive attitude towards new challenges.
- **Developmental Action 2:** Support leaders in navigating organizational change by providing the tools, training, and guidance they need to lead their teams through transitions effectively.

Performance Management

- **Developmental Action 1:** Set high performance expectations for leaders and provide the necessary support and resources to help them achieve these standards.
- **Developmental Action 2:** Conduct regular performance reviews with leaders, offering constructive feedback and identifying opportunities for growth and development.

Innovation

- **Developmental Action 1:** Challenge leaders to think creatively and explore new approaches to solving problems, fostering an environment where innovation is encouraged and valued.
- **Developmental Action 2:** Reward leaders who propose and implement innovative ideas that contribute to the organization's success, reinforcing a culture of continuous improvement.

Section 5: Coach

Strategic Mentorship

- **Developmental Action 1:** Provide high-level mentorship to other leaders, guiding them in aligning their goals and strategies with the broader organizational vision.
- **Developmental Action 2:** Help leaders navigate complex challenges by offering insights and advice based on your experience and understanding of the organization's strategy.

Leadership Development

- **Developmental Action 1:** Actively work on developing the leadership capabilities of others by providing access to leadership training programs and resources.
- **Developmental Action 2:** Prepare leaders for higher levels of responsibility by involving them in decision-making processes and exposing them to strategic initiatives.

Systems Thinking

- **Developmental Action 1:** Coach leaders to understand the interdependencies within the organization, helping them see how their decisions impact other areas of the business.
- **Developmental Action 2:** Encourage leaders to think in terms of systems and processes, considering the broader implications of their actions on the organization as a whole.

Executive Presence

- **Developmental Action 1:** Help leaders develop the communication skills and presence needed to influence at the highest levels of the organization.
- **Developmental Action 2:** Provide feedback to leaders on their executive presence, offering specific advice on how they can enhance their impact and effectiveness.

Succession Planning

- **Developmental Action 1:** Guide leaders in identifying and developing potential successors, ensuring a strong leadership pipeline for the organization.
- **Developmental Action 2:** Work with leaders to create and implement effective succession plans that align with the long-term goals of the organization.

Section 6: Celebrate

Recognition

- **Developmental Action 1:** Regularly acknowledge the achievements and contributions of other leaders, both privately and publicly, reinforcing their value to the organization.
- **Developmental Action 2:** Create opportunities to celebrate the successes of leaders in visible ways, such as through awards, recognition programs, or public acknowledgments.

Appreciation

- **Developmental Action 1:** Express gratitude regularly for the efforts and contributions of other leaders, fostering a positive and motivating work environment.
- **Developmental Action 2:** Ensure that leaders feel valued and appreciated by acknowledging their hard work and dedication in both formal and informal settings.

Public Acknowledgment

- **Developmental Action 1:** Make a point to publicly celebrate the successes of leaders, using these moments to inspire others and build morale within the leadership team.
- **Developmental Action 2:** Use public acknowledgment to highlight exemplary leadership behaviors and outcomes, setting a standard for others to aspire to.

Team Spirit

- **Developmental Action 1:** Promote a sense of camaraderie and collective pride among leaders by organizing team-building activities and events that bring the leadership team together.
- **Developmental Action 2:** Encourage leaders to support and celebrate each other's successes, reinforcing a collaborative and positive team culture.

Positive Reinforcement

- **Developmental Action 1:** Use celebration as a tool to reinforce desired behaviors and outcomes among leaders, making recognition a regular part of your leadership culture.
- **Developmental Action 2:** Ensure that positive reinforcement is consistently applied, creating an environment where leaders are motivated to achieve excellence.

Incorporating these developmental actions for leading other leaders strengthens the organization's leadership foundation by fostering a culture of inclusivity, empowerment, and continuous growth. By focusing on strategic relationship building, emotional intelligence, and cultural competence, leaders are better equipped to guide their teams through challenges and opportunities. The E3C3 framework's Six Core Elements—Embrace, Empower, Engage, Challenge, Coach, and Celebrate—provide a structured approach to cultivating leadership excellence. By implementing these actions, organizations can create a more cohesive, motivated, and high-performing leadership team that drives long-term success.